The Truth about
SALVATION

Dedicated to

Larry Stutzman

A dedicated servant of Christ;
A genuine encouragement to me

TABLE OF CONTENTS

Preface 9
1. God Is a Loving Creator 13
2. Man Is a Rebellious Creature 23
3. God Is a Righteous Judge 35
4. God Is a Gracious Redeemer 43
5. Jesus Is a Divine Savior. 53
6. Jesus Is a Human Savior 63
7. Salvation Is by Faith Alone 75
8. Salvation Is a Life Changer 85
9. Salvation Is Eternally Secure 95
10. Christians Have a Glorious Destiny 105
11. Christians Have an Evangelistic Obligation 119
12. Christianity Is a Certain Faith. 129
Conclusion 143

PREFACE

This is the first book to be released in GoodBirth Ministries' *Truth About Series*. This new book series deals with topics of deep significance and abiding interest to Bible-believing Christians. The studies are designed for serious Christians who love God's Word and want to better understand both it and the Christian worldview arising from it. The theme governing this series is: "Sanctifying God's People through God's Truth." Our undergirding theme verse is taken from Christ's prayer regarding his followers:

"Sanctify them in the truth; Your word is truth" (John 17:17)

The Point of the *About Truth* Series

The *Truth About Series* offers succinct, biblically-based, and carefully-structured studies specifically designed for either personal or small group Bible studies. Not only do the chapters breakdown the material in logical chunks, but at the end of each chapter we present two types of study questions:

- Review Questions that assist the reader in better comprehending the core issues dealt with in the chapter.
- Discussion Questions that promote further group reflection on the topic beyond that which is presented.

Unlike many Christian study guides the books in this series will deal seriously with the issues at hand, rather than skimming the surface, stating the obvious, or providing cute stories. The very issues studied merit due consideration because of their significance for the Christian worldview. We will assume the reader's deep interest in understanding the Bible and its relationship to the topic being analyzed.

The Significance of the *About Truth* Series

Our desire is to help remedy a problem that has plagued God's people from time immemorial and which is especially problematic today. God warned through Hosea: "My people are destroyed for lack of knowledge." In fact, he informed his Old Testament people that they went "into exile for their lack of knowledge" because their "honorable men" were "famished" and the multitude of the people were parched with thirst" (Isa 5:13). The writer of Hebrews chastises first-century Christians:

> "You have become dull of hearing. For though by this time you ought to be teachers, you have need again for someone to teach you the elementary principles of the oracles of God, and you have come to need milk and not solid food. For everyone who partakes only of milk is not accustomed to the word of righteousness, for he is an infant. But solid food is for the mature, who because of practice have their senses trained to discern good and evil." (Heb 5:11–14)

Christianity is a revealed religion established on divinely-inspired truth claims. As the apostle Paul states: "For this reason we also constantly thank God that when you received the word of God which you heard from us, you accepted it not as the word of men, but for what it really is, the word of God" (1 Thess 2:13). Thus, we firmly believe that "all Scripture is inspired by God and profitable for teaching" (2 Tim 3:16; cp. 1 Cor 2:4).

God's word exercises a significant influence on the whole Christian life and experience. We become Christians through the instrumentality of his word: "for you have been born again not of seed which is perishable but imperishable, that is, through the living and enduring word of God" (1 Pet 1:23). Indeed, "faith comes from hearing, and hearing by the word of Christ" (Rom 10:17). Because of this Christians must "hold fast the word" unless they have "believed in vain" (1 Cor 15:2)

The role of God's word does not end with our new birth. Indeed, we are to grow and develop spiritually by means of that word: "like newborn babies, long for the pure milk of the word, so that by it you may grow in respect to salvation" (1 Pet 2:2). Paul speaks of Christ's love for the church in Ephesians 5:26 where he adds: "that He might sanctify her, having cleansed her by the washing of water with the word. Hence, Jesus' prayer to God in our behalf: "sanctify them in the truth; Your word is truth" (John 17:17). Therefore Christians must "let the word of Christ richly dwell within you" (Col 3:16) for "the word of truth" is "the power of God" (2 Cor 6:7).

God has given us the Scriptures "for teaching for reproof, for correction, for training in righteousness, so that the man of God may be adequate, equipped for every good work" (2 Tim 3:17). Therefore, the

Christian must study and understand the Bible, for we are commanded to "be diligent to present yourself approved to God as a workman who does not need to be ashamed, accurately handling the word of truth" (2 Tim 2:15).

Then having learned God's word the child of God must apply it to his life, family, society, and culture. Paul insists that you must "speak the word of God without fear" (Php 1:14). He urges the believer to hold "fast the faithful word which is in accordance with the teaching, so that he will be able both to exhort in sound doctrine and to refute those who contradict" (Tit 1:9). As a committed Christian you are called to take "every thought captive to the obedience of Christ" (2 Cor 10:5).

From these several verses we can see the incredible significance of God's word on the Christian's life. Our *Truth About Series* is designed to minister to those Christians who are committed to understanding the Bible and the Christian worldview better.

Chapter 1
GOD IS A LOVING CREATOR

As we open our study of The Truth about Salvation, we must begin literally at the beginning: we must start in the first book of the Bible, Genesis.

Genesis is the book of beginnings, and for our purposes we will focus on its presentation of the beginning of the world, of man, and the revelation of God's goodness to man. In order to properly understand our spiritual hope in a God-given salvation we must recognize our historical context in a God-created world. Neither Christianity nor salvation can be abstracted from the real world. Christianity is not a magical and mystical faith, but an historical and supernatural one.

God Creates the World

As Bible-believing Christians we do not hold that the universe mysteriously exploded into being from out of nowhere around 13 billion years ago. Nor do we believe that life evolved from the primordial ooze by chance processes beginning about 4 billion years ago. Nor do we believe man finally arose from animals by slow, gradual, random genetic mutations 2.5 million years ago. In short, we do not believe the world and life originated by the impersonal forces proposed in evolutionary theory.

The world, life, and man were created by an infinite, personal, righteous God. He alone accounts for all reality (see ch. 12 for discussion of this point). Because of this, we believe the world and life have meaning, value, and purpose. This is why we must begin our inquiry into salvation by God's grace while first focusing on our creation by God's greatness. We do not receive salvation as a result of an exploding universe, but as a result of a loving Creator.

Genesis is truly the foundational book of all Scripture, for it presents the origin of all things. And it presents that origin in terms of a personal, good, and righteous God. The rational universe is rooted in a rational God. In majestic simplicity the Bible opens with this astounding declaration: "In the beginning God created the heavens and the earth." These few words present us with the power, wisdom, and glory of God as the Creator. Thus, the God who saves sinners is the majestic Creator.

In Genesis 1 we find the historical account of creation. And that creation account is dominated by the presence and activity of God Almighty. We not only see his name stated in the opening verse, but it appears thirty-five times in its thirty-one verses. In fact, it is in every verse except for verses 13, 19, 23, 30.

The name used of God throughout Genesis 1 is the Hebrew word *elohim*. It is actually the plural of *el*, which means "powerful, mighty." The meaning of this plural form is called either the intensive plural or the plural of majesty. It underscores God's manifold strength and majesty, and serves as a most appropriate presentation of the one who will be creating the entire universe in the following account.

The opening verse of Genesis is one of the best known verses in all of Scripture. Genesis 1:1 opens with the bold declaration that all the universe was created by God. Not only so, but throughout Scripture this is repeatedly reaffirmed, not only of God but even of God's Son, Jesus Christ the Lord and Savior. For example, we see this in: Exodus 20:11; 31:17; Psalm 33:6; 89:11; 90:2; 115:15; 146:6; Isaiah 40:26; 42:5; 45:12; John 1:3, 10; Acts 4:24; 14:15; 17:24; 1 Corinthians 8:6; Colossians 1:16–17; Hebrews 1:2, 10; 11:3; Revelation 4:11; 10:6; and 14:7.

Furthermore, the Bible always states that our powerful God alone created the universe. Nehemiah 9:6 is one of those glorious pronouncements: "You alone are the LORD. / You have made the heavens, / The heaven of heavens with all their host, / The earth and all that is on it, / The seas and all that is in them. / You give life to all of them / And the heavenly host bows down before You."

Because a good God created the universe, the universe is originally "very good" (Gen.1:31). In fact, its goodness is declared all through the creational process, as we see in just two samples: Genesis 1:3–4a reads: "Then God said, 'Let there be light'; and there was light. God saw that the light was good." Genesis 1:10: "God called the dry land earth, and the gathering of the waters He called seas; and God saw that it was good."[1]

---

[1] Only Day 2 lacks this divine appreciation formula, "it was good." This is because though God divides the water by creating the "firmament" which separates the waters into lower and upper realms on Day 2, he is not finished with the waters until Day 3. Then he separates the land and the water, forming

God Creates Man

The Bible opens in its first chapter with the majestic march of six days.[2] In Genesis 1 we read the record of God's unfolding creative process as it leads to its climax in the creation of man (Gen 1:26–28). Man is the very goal of creation, and its high point. In fact, though it necessarily mentions the creation of the starry heavens (Gen 1:1, 14–16), the creation record intentionally focuses on a small part of the universe: the earth, its flora and fauna . . . and man (Gen 1:2–13, 17–30). And even the creation of the sun, moon, and stars is for the purpose of giving light on earth the special arena of God's creative work (Gen 1:14–16).

What is more, man is not only the very goal and purpose of the whole creational process, but he is also God's highest creature. He alone of all creation is made in the image and likeness of God (Gen 1:26). And this marvelous truth is emphasized in a double statement: "God created man in His own image, in the image of God He created him" (Gen 1:27a).

Not only so, but man's creation is presented as the result of a careful, deliberative process within God's Triune being: "Then God said, 'Let Us make man in Our image, according to Our likeness; and let them rule over the fish of the sea and over the birds of the sky and over the cattle and over all the earth, and over every creeping thing that creeps on the earth'" (Gen 1:26). Genesis emphasizes that man's creation is the most special act among God's works.

God is of such great power that we might wonder: Why did he take six days to create the world? Does he not have the power to create it all at once? After all, when the Psalmist summarizes God's creative activity he presents it as requiring no more of God's energy than a mere breath: "By the word of the LORD the heavens were made, / And by the breath of His mouth all their host" (Psa 33:6; cp. Psa 148:5; Heb 11:3; 2 Pet 3:5). This, of course, matches the Genesis record which repeatedly and simply states: "God said" (Gen 1:3, 6, 11, 14, 20, 22, 24). And this is frequently followed by the declaration: "and it was so" (Gen 1:7, 9, 11, 15, 24).

---

what he only then calls "the Seas" (1:9-10). Then, and only then, does he declare his completed work with the water "good" (1:10).

[2] For a thorough presentation and defense of Six-day Creation, see: Kenneth L. Gentry, Jr., *As It is Written: The Genesis Account: Literal or Literary?* (Green Forest, Ark., Master, 2016).

Indeed, elsewhere David poetically pictures the creation as performed by the snapping of God's fingers, as it were. In Psalm 8 we read: "when I consider Your heavens, the work of Your fingers" (Psa 8:3a). David portrays the creation of the stellar universe as a very small thing for God: it does not require his back and arms, but merely his fingers.

So then, why does God take six days to create the world? We discover elsewhere that he did so *as a model for man*, his special image. The Fourth Commandment states:

> "Six days you shall labor and do all your work, but the seventh day is a sabbath of the LORD your God; in it you shall not do any work, you or your son or your daughter, your male or your female servant or your cattle or your sojourner who stays with you. For in six days the LORD made the heavens and the earth, the sea and all that is in them, and rested on the seventh day; therefore the LORD blessed the sabbath day and made it holy." (Exo 20:9–11)

Thus, God set the pattern for man: he worked six days and rested one, so his image should reflect him and labor for six days and rest one. As God's image man is to exercise dominion over all the creatures of the earth, thereby reflecting God's superior, ultimate dominion over them (Gen 1:26–30).

God Is Good to Man

In the original creation record we discover not only that God creates a good world and man to populate it (Gen 1:31), but that he is especially good to man.

In the very historical context of creating Adam and Eve we read: "God blessed them" (Gen 1:28a). And though he also blesses the animals (Gen 1:22), he goes further with man by giving him dominion over all other creatures: "Let them rule over the fish of the sea and over the birds of the sky and over the cattle and over all the earth, and over every creeping thing that creeps on the earth" (Gen 1:26b, 28b).

David marvels at this glorious fact in Psalm 8:4–6: "What is man that You take thought of him, / And the son of man that You care for him? / Yet You have made him a little lower than God, / And You crown him with glory and majesty! / You make him to rule over the works of Your hands; / You have put all things under his feet." When he views the smallness of man in relation to the largeness of the stellar sky (Psa 8:2), he is amazed at all that God has granted to man.

In Genesis 2 Moses presents us with a more detailed focus on God's creating Adam and Eve, a focus providing us significant details that we do not see in the terse statement in Genesis 1:26–28. Here we discover that God creates man by a different means from his creating the animals.

When God creates the animals he merely commands "let there be," and this is followed by the instant result "and it was so" (Gen 1:24). In man's creation, however, we find God's special care and deeply personal involvement: "Then the LORD God formed man of dust from the ground, and breathed into his nostrils the breath of life; and man became a living being" (Gen 2:7). This is very personal and affectionate.

Not only so, but the Lord specially places man in a beautiful garden to begin his task of world dominion: "The LORD God planted a garden toward the east, in Eden; and there He placed the man whom He had formed. Out of the ground the LORD God caused to grow every tree that is pleasing to the sight and good for food; the tree of life also in the midst of the garden, and the tree of the knowledge of good and evil" (Gen 2:8–9).

The Scriptures repeatedly emphasize God's goodness to man — even after the Fall in Eden. After God's judgment on sin in the Flood, we read: "While the earth remains, / Seedtime and harvest, / And cold and heat, / And summer and winter, / And day and night / Shall not cease" (Gen 8:22). Jesus declares of God's providence in the world that "He causes His sun to rise on the evil and the good, and sends rain on the righteous and the unrighteous" (Matt 5:45). Paul preaches in Lystra: "He did not leave Himself without witness, in that He did good and gave you rains from heaven and fruitful seasons, satisfying your hearts with food and gladness" (Acts 14:17). See also Job 5:10; Psalm 65:9–13; 104:13; 147:8; Jeremiah 5:24.

This agrees with the psalmist who praises God because "the earth is full of the lovingkindness of the LORD" (Psa 33:5b; cp. Psa 119:64). In Psalm 36:6 David praises God: "you preserve man and beast." Psalms 104 declares God's goodness to all of creation. For instance, in Psalm 104: 14–15 we read: "He causes the grass to grow for the cattle, / And vegetation for the labor of man, / So that he may bring forth food from the earth, / And wine which makes man's heart glad, / So that he may make his face glisten with oil, / And food which sustains man's heart."

As his highest creature, man must recognize that "every good thing given and every perfect gift is from above, coming down from the Father of lights, with whom there is no variation or shifting shadow" (Jms 1:17). He must understand that it is "God who richly supplies us with all things to enjoy" (1 Tim 6:17). Because of this "there is nothing better for a man than to eat and drink and tell himself that his labor is good. This also I have seen that it is from the hand of God" (Eccl 2:25).

In fact, God does good to fallen man with a view to saving him. Paul states in Romans 2:4: "Do you think lightly of the riches of His kindness and tolerance and patience, not knowing that the kindness of God leads you to repentance?" At Athens he preaches this same theme: "He Himself gives to all people life and breath and all things. . . . Therefore having overlooked the times of ignorance, God is now declaring to men that all people everywhere should repent" (Acts 17:25, 30).

God Is Perfectly Righteous

The God who creates man and gives him all good things, is perfect and righteous. The Bible repeatedly speaks of God's absolute righteousness, making such statements as:

"The Rock! His work is perfect, / For all His ways are just; / A God of faithfulness and without injustice, / Righteous and upright is He" (Deut 32:4).

"As for God, His way is blameless" (Psa 18:30a; 2 Sam 22:31).

"Your righteousness is like the mountains of God; Your judgments are like a great deep" (Psa 36:6).

"Your righteousness, O God, reaches to the heavens" (Psa 71:19a).

"The ways of the LORD are right" (Hos 14:9).

"The LORD is righteous within her; / He will do no injustice. / Every morning He brings His justice to light; / He does not fail. / But the unjust knows no shame" (Zeph 3:5).

Jesus prays to God calling him "righteous Father" (John 17:25).

Consequently, righteousness is a constantly manifested attribute of God. He always acts righteously, for "Your righteousness is an everlasting righteousness" (Psa 119:142a). "He loves righteousness and justice" (Psa 33:5). In fact, God delights in acting righteously: "I am the LORD who exercises lovingkindness, justice and righteousness on earth; for I delight in these things" (Jer 9:24). As a result, the saints praise him: "Great and marvelous are Your works, / O Lord God, the Almighty; / Righteous and true are Your ways, / King of the nations!" (Rev 15:3).

God Expects Righteousness in Us

Righteousness is an inherent attribute of God, a specific, ever-present characteristic or quality of his nature. Because of this, he is righteous at all times and in all his ways. As a righteous Creator he creates man in his image (Gen 1:26–28) as a moral creature (Gen 2:17). Man is created as morally "upright" being possessing a moral consciousness (Eccl 7:29).

Paul associates the image of God with righteousness when he urge Christians to "put on the new self, which in the likeness of God has been created in righteousness and holiness of the truth" (Eph 4:24; cp. Col 3:9–10). He even notes that pagans have an instinctive awareness of morality: "when Gentiles who do not have the Law do instinctively the things of the Law, these, not having the Law, are a law to themselves, in that they show the work of the Law written in their hearts, their conscience bearing witness and their thoughts alternately accusing or else defending them" (Rom 2:14–15).

But God does not leave man to determine his own moral standards. Rather he gives us his righteous Law so that we might know true righteousness and might properly reflect his image. He begins this in Eden by presenting a moral test to Adam in Eden to see if he will allow God to determine good and evil, or whether he will arrogate that responsibility to himself:

> "The LORD God commanded the man, saying, 'From any tree of the garden you may eat freely; but from the tree of the knowledge of good and evil you shall not eat, for in the day that you eat from it you will surely die.'" (Gen 2:16–17)

Satan sees this test for what it is, and so tempts Eve accordingly. He entices her by holding out the prospect of her sitting as God, determining good and evil: "For God knows that in the day you eat from it your eyes will be opened, and you will be like God, knowing [i.e., determining] good and evil" (Gen 3:5).

From the beginning, therefore, our righteous God expects righteousness from us. And he continues calling us to righteousness throughout Scripture and throughout history. As he delivers Israel from bondage and establishes her as a nation he charges her to righteous conduct: "You shall be blameless before the LORD your God" (Deut 18:13).

To guide Israel in the paths of righteousness he reveals his Law to her: "Beware that you do not forget the LORD your God by not keeping His commandments and His ordinances and His statutes which I am commanding you today" (Deut 8:11). He givers her his Law in order to serve as the foundation of her national existence. Therefore, we read that Moses challenges Israel: "what great nation is there that has statutes and judgments as righteous as this whole law which I am setting before you today?" (Deut 4:8).

The Lord does not give his righteous Law to Israel as a distinctive for her alone. He expressly states that Israel must live in terms of his Law's statutes *in order to be an example to the nations*: "keep and do them, for that is your wisdom and your understanding in the sight of the nations" (Deut 4:6). And this continues into the New Testament for Paul notes in Romans 3:19: "we know that whatever the Law says, it speaks to those who are under the Law, so that *every mouth* may be closed and all the *world may* become accountable to God."

Just a few verses after declaring the whole world under God's Law Paul rhetorically asks: "Do we then nullify the Law through faith? May it never be! On the contrary, we establish the Law" (Rom 3:31). Later he teaches Timothy that the Law continues as binding upon men as necessary for curtailing sin and crime, and that it is a continuing function of "sound teaching, according to the glorious gospel":

> "We know that the Law is good, if one uses it lawfully, realizing the fact that law is not made for a righteous person, but for those who are lawless and rebellious, for the ungodly and sinners, for the unholy and profane, for those who kill their fathers or mothers, for murderers and immoral men and homosexuals and kidnappers and liars and perjurers, and whatever else is contrary to sound teaching, according to the glorious gospel of the blessed God, with which I have been entrusted."

Because of this righteous standard of morality revealed by God for Israel and the world, we find recurring calls to righteousness in Scripture. For instance, Jesus calls down blessings upon those who seek righteousness: "blessed are those who hunger and thirst for righteousness" (Matt 5:6). And he promises as a consequence that if we "seek first His kingdom and His righteousness. . . all these things [i.e., food and clothing] will be added to you."

The Lord even calls his followers to strict righteousness by commanding them: "you are to be perfect, as your heavenly Father is perfect" (Matt 5:48). Our standard for this perfect righteousness is his Law, for Paul declares: "the Law is holy, and the commandment is holy and righteous and good" (Rom 7:12; cp. 7:16; 1 Tim 1:8).

Conclusion

The Christian worldview, which is rooted in Scripture, recognizes God as the Creator who made man in his own image. This necessarily entails man's being a moral creature. We find the record of creation and of man's earliest days in Genesis 1–2. There we learn that God creates a "very good" world and is good to man in giving him a happy, peaceful, wholesome, and productive environment.

God is a perfectly righteous God who expects man to live righteously in his world. Therefore, he gives man a righteous Law to guide him in his behavior. The Law is given to Israel to guide her in her own national conduct. But she is to be a model of righteousness so that the nations would adopt God's Law as their standard. And God's Law prevails even today as the universal standard of righteousness. Jesus calls upon his followers to strive to be perfect, because God is perfect.

But this study is about salvation. Salvation from what? We know that something is wrong with man. We must next consider man as a rebellious creature. Especially since God is a perfectly righteous God who expects his moral creature to reflect him. This will be considered in the next chapter.

REVIEW QUESTIONS FOR DISCUSSION

These questions deal directly with the material in this chapter. The answers can be found in the chapter.

1. List some ways in which the biblical account of creation demonstrates that God is a loving Creator.
2. What name of God is used in the Genesis 1 creation account? What does it mean? How is it significant for understanding salvation?

3. Genesis 2 provides a detailed account of the creation of man, which is only summarily stated in Genesis 1. How does this account impact our understanding of salvation?
4. How does the creation of man differ from that of animals? How does this emphasize God's loving concern for man?
5. How is the fact that man is the goal of God's creative work helpful for understanding the doctrine of salvation?
6. Explain how Scripture repeatedly shows God's goodness to man in creation even beyond the record in Genesis.
7. Man is the image of God who therefore reflects God. God is perfectly righteous. How is God's righteousness significant for understanding what he expects of man in the world, and how does this affect our understanding of salvation?
8. Discuss God's test of Adam in Genesis 2:16–17. What is the particular test designed to confirm? How will this lead to the necessity of God's saving activity?
9. God's Law is given to Israel. How do we know that it was not given solely for Israel but through her to the world?
10. What is the standard of righteousness to which God and Christ call us?

STRETCHING FURTHER

These questions are designed to promote further group reflection on the topic beyond that which is presented in the chapter above.

1. Is the biblical account of creation compatible with evolutionary theory? What are some key differences between the views?
2. What are some moral implications of evolutionary theory regarding the function of man in the world?
3. Why is it a good idea to start a study of salvation in the book of Genesis?
4. Discuss the image of God in man. What are some of the features of God's image in man?
5. Are angels created in God's image? Why do you believe this? Explain the implications of your answer.

Chapter 2
MAN IS A REBELLIOUS CREATURE

As we noted in our previous study, God is righteous and he expects righteousness in his highest creature, man. But the world that we live in is obviously not a righteous one. Something is wrong with man — radically wrong. And we must understand this if we are to grasp the *Truth about Salvation*, and the necessity of the gospel of Jesus Christ. We must recognize that men are lost sinners who must seek true salvation from their sin.

Let us consider man's rebellion in terms of its: historical origin (Adam's fall into sin), radical effect (man's total depravity), debilitating consequence (man's inability to please God), and tragic significance (man's record before God). Once we do this we should be very much aware of the sinner's deep and desperate need of God's saving mercies.

Man's Fall

As Solomon states: "God made men upright, but they have sought out many devices" (Eccl 7:29). This certainly reflects the biblical record regarding both man's original creation and his current situation. Man did not originally come into this world as a corrupt sinner. He *became* that way as a consequence of something occurring early in his life in God's newly-created world. And we have the historical record of that also in Genesis, the book of beginnings.

Adam and his fall

As we noted in the previous chapter, when God tenderly creates Adam he places him in the Garden of Eden to enjoy a good environment and personal fellowship with God. But the Lord places him there as a free moral agent and presents him with a moral test designed to confirm him in righteousness. With all that God provides for him, would Adam let God be God, determining good and evil? Or would he be tempted to arrogate that prerogative to himself? Tragically, the latter result prevails.

The Genesis record does not tell us everything we might like to know about Adam and his fall. For instance, it does not inform us how much time passes after his creation before he is tempted and falls.[1] Nor does it tell us about Satan's fall which must be prior to Adam's.

But the Genesis account does tell us what we need to know:
- Adam is created directly by God (Gen 2:7)
- He is created morally upright (Gen 1:26–27)
- He is placed in a perfect environment (Gen 2:15)
- He is a free moral agent (he could sin and die, Gen 2:17)
- He is tested by God (Gen 2:16–17)

Yes, despite God's goodness, he rebels against his Maker and falls from his high moral condition. And the rest, as they say, is history.

In Genesis 1 and 2 we read of God's loving creation of Adam and his wonderful provision for him. And in Genesis 3 we find the basic record of his fall and God's response to it. Whereas God directly commands Adam not to eat of the tree, the serpent (indwelt by Satan, 2 Cor 11:3; Rev 12:9; 20:2) approaches Eve to cast doubt on God's goodness: Eve "saw that the tree was *good* for food" (Gen 3:6).[2] Satan is leading her to decide that God is actually not good, in that he is keeping back something good from them. In fact, he specifically states that God did not want them to be like him (despite being created in his image), implying that he is denying them something they could enjoy (Gen 3:5).

---

[1] Adam's temptation and fall probably occur not long after his creation. We may surmise this from the fact that he is commanded to multiply (Gen 1:28) and yet he has not yet produced children by the time of his fall (Gen 3:16; 4:1). And though we cannot be sure, his fall may occur on the eighth day, the day after God's rest on the seventh. This may be hinted at in that circumcision (which represents the cutting away of the filth of the heart, Deut 10:16; 30:6; Jer 4:4; cp. Lev 26:41; Jer 9:26; Eze 44:7, 9; Acts 7:51) occurs on the eighth day (Gen 17:12; 21:4; Lev 12:3; Luke 1:59; Phil 3:5). Other eighth day ceremonies may also indicate this (Exo 22:30; Lev 15:29; 22:27; Num 29:35).

[2] Some hold that Eve alters God's command by adding "or touch it" (Gen 3:3). The word for "touch," however, does not speak of the mere handling of the fruit. It is a word that suggests taking it for one's own, with the view of eating it. Consequently, this shows that she fully understood God's prohibition. See: E. J. Young, *Genesis 3* (Edinburgh: Banner of Truth, 1966), 30–31.

So then, when Eve sees that the tree is "good for food, and that it was a delight to the eyes" (Gen 3:6), she takes and eats its fruit. Then she gives to her husband who follows her in her rebellion against God's direct command. This presents us with a most remarkable state of affairs. We need to note exactly what transpires here.

Adam is the head of Eve (Gen 2:18; cf. 1 Tim 2:11–13). But both of them are created in God's image, so that they both are to exercise dominion over the animals (Gen 1:26–27). In fact, Adam "names" the animals, showing his dominion over them (Gen 2:20). Nevertheless, in the fall narrative we find the inversion of God's created order. Under the influence of Satan, the serpent speaks (which animals cannot naturally do, since they are not in God's image[3]). Then he uses his speech to exercise dominion over Eve, leading her to exercise dominion over Adam. Sin thereby enters into the human race.

Immediately after the fall, God confronts Adam with his sin (Gen 3:8–12). Whereupon he curses not only the serpent that Satan uses as his instrument (Gen 3:14–15), but also Eve who must now bear children with great difficulty (Gen 3:16) and Adam who must now labor over a resistant soil (Gen 3:17–18). And now death enters the world to overshadow all of man's labor (Gen 3:19). Adam's fall not only has moral and spiritual implications, but also physical consequences.

Adam as our representative

Adam is an individual, but he is an individual who represents others and acts in their behalf. In him we all were tested and fell, much like God's people being tested and approved on the basis of Christ's work. Paul drives home the representative role of Adam, paralleling him in this regard to Jesus, who is called the "last Adam" (1 Cor 15:45) or "the second man" (1 Cor 15:47). And in drawing this parallel, he shows that the whole human race is polluted with sin because of Adam's fall:

> "Therefore, just as through one man sin entered into the world, and death through sin, and so death spread to all men, because all sinned — for until the Law sin was in the world, but sin is not imputed when there is no law. Nevertheless death reigned from

---

[3] The image of God apparently involves rational speech because the context of the statement that man is God's image includes frequent references to God speaking and calling (Gen 1:3, 5, 6, 8, 10, 11, 14, 20, 22, 24, 26, 28, 29).

Adam until Moses, even over those who had not sinned in the likeness of the offense of Adam, who is a type of Him who was to come." (Rom 5:12–14; cp. 1 Cor 15:22)

The 1784 edition of *The New-England Primer* poetically captures this truth in: "In Adam's fall, / we sinned all."[4]

Elsewhere Paul states that "all are under sin" (Rom 3:9) and "all have sinned and fall short of the glory of God" (Rom 3:23). He declares that "the Scripture has shut up everyone under sin" (Gal 3:22). This truth matches the statements of Scripture elsewhere:

"There is no man who does not sin." (2 Chron 6:36)

"The LORD has looked down from heaven upon the sons of men / To see if there are any who understand, / Who seek after God. / They have all turned aside, together they have become corrupt; / There is no one who does good, not even one." (Psa 14:2–3)

"In Your sight no man living is righteous." (Psa 143:2)

"Indeed, there is not a righteous man on earth who continually does good and who never sins." (Eccl 7:20)

"All of us like sheep have gone astray, / Each of us has turned to his own way." (Isa 53:6)

"There is no one good except God alone." (Mark 10:18)

And man's sinfulness is not something he learns in due time. Rather he is born with it; in fact, depravity infects him from the first moment of his existence, from his very conception. David's confession of sin notes that not only is man born a sinner, but he is conceived as a sinner: "Behold, I was brought forth in iniquity, / And in sin my mother conceived me" (Psa 51:5).

Because of this, Paul can well state that all men are "by nature children of wrath" (Eph 2:3). This explains why God can say of man: "the intent of man's heart is evil from his youth" (Gen 8:21). And why David can lament: "The wicked are estranged from the womb; / These who speak lies go astray from birth" (Psa 58:3).

---

[4] Perhaps one of the best known verses found in this Puritan primer is: "Now I lay me down to sleep, / I pray thee, Lord, my soul to keep; / If I should die before I wake, / I pray thee, Lord, my soul to take." Other short verses include: "As runs the Glass, / Man's life doth pass" and "My Book and Heart / Shall never part."

Clearly then, in the biblical outlook all men are fallen sinners. And they are sinners despite God's goodness. They are rebels against a noble and glorious king, the Lord God Almighty. Men must be brought to this realization before they can know the *Truth about Salvation*. And the Christian must understand the gravity of this truth before he can realize the importance of witnessing to others about their need of Christ.

Man's Depravity

Not only does Scripture teach that Adam fell and that all men fell in him so that all become sinners in the sight of God. But it also warns that all men are "totally depraved." But what does this mean? And where does the Bible teach it?

What "total depravity" does not mean

By "total depravity" we do not mean that all men are as evil as they can be, that all men display their sin to the fullest extent possible, i.e., totally. This is patently not so. Satan is certainly the epitome of evil and as sinful as he can be, but not man himself.

In fact, we know of notorious sinners who are far more sinful than the unsaved "little old lady from Pasadena." We can think of such infamous men as Nero Caesar, Atilla the Hun, Vlad Dracula, Tomas de Torquemada, Adolf Hitler, Joseph Stalin, Mao Tse Tung, Idi Amin, Kim Il Sung, and Osama bin Laden. These are but a few men who inflict great harm on broader society.

And even on a more local level, we can think of many infamous criminals who act alone for their own evil desires. We can list Jack the Ripper, Charles Manson, Jim Jones, Ted Bundy, John Wayne Gacy, Ted Kaczynski, and others. These exercise their sinfulness more fully than your unregenerate next-door neighbor.

Nor does total depravity mean that men cannot act in *any* relatively good way toward others. Or that he can *never* do anything whatsoever that is formally right in terms of God's Law. For instance, anytime we do not murder someone, we externally and formally keep God's good law in that regard. We keep God's command: "You shall not murder" (Exo 12:13).

So then, let us consider:

What "total depravity" does mean

Though the phrase "total depravity" confuses many who surmise that it means absolute depravity, it actually means three things:

1. The totality of mankind is corrupted by sin. That is, though man is not as *intensively* evil as possible, he is *extensively* evil throughout the whole human race.
2. The totality of the individual's being is sinful in its every part. That is, man's sin does not affect man only partly, but infects his heart, soul, mind, and strength.
3. The totality of man's endeavors are infected by sin. That is, sin affects every sphere of his life. Men are individually sinful in themselves, as well as corporately sinful in society.

But we must also recognize an important implication of total depravity, and that is: man's total *inability*.

Man's Inability

Man's total depravity inexorably leads to his total inability. This speaks of his inability to do what is *truly and fully* good in the eyes of God. But before we can properly understand this doctrine of man's inability, we must first recognize the nature of true good, i.e., good that is acceptable to God.

That which is truly and fully good is the thought, talk, and walk that meet up to the three-fold evaluation of Scripture. That is, for any thought, word, or deed to be good *in the sight of God*, it must have as its *goal* the glory of God (1 Cor 10:31), as its *motive* faith in God (Rom 14:23), and as its *standard* the Law of God (Rom 7:12). Theologians speak of this as the "triadic structure of biblical ethics." That is, all three angles are needed in order to pass God's ultimate evaluation; no one angle can stand alone.

Because of the triangular nature of ethics, Isaiah can state regarding deeds that many might approve: "all our righteous deeds are like a filthy garment" (Isa 64:6). This is because man's sinful acts flow from deep within his being to permeate every aspect of his life. Jesus confirms this when he teaches that "out of the heart come evil thoughts, murders, adulteries, fornications, thefts, false witness, slanders" (Matt 15:19). In fact, because of this Jesus also teaches that "men loved the darkness rather than the Light, for their deeds were evil" (John 3:19).

How can we expect true good to flow out of fallen man who is deemed in Scripture to be "dead in trespasses and sins" (Eph 2:1)? John dogmatically declares that "he who has the Son has the life; he who does not have the Son of God does not have the life" (1 John 5:12). God says: "the heart is more deceitful than all else / And is desperately sick" (Jer 17:9). Because of man's spiritual deadness, Jesus teaches that "unless one is born again he cannot see the kingdom of God" (John 3:3).

With this understanding of man's depravity and the nature of the good, we can now focus on man's total inability. Many verses declare the sinner *unable* to please God. Consider the following samples.

Through the prophet Jeremiah God asks: "Can the Ethiopian change his skin / Or the leopard his spots? / Then you also can do good / Who are accustomed to doing evil" (Jer 13:23).

Jesus declares man's inability when he teaches: "a good tree cannot produce bad fruit, nor can a bad tree produce good fruit" (Matt 7:18). What he is saying here is that those who are not born again into a new life by God's grace are like bad trees that *cannot* bring forth good, acceptable fruit.

Paul agrees with this moral and spiritual inability of man before God: "the mind set on the flesh is hostile toward God; for it does not subject itself to the law of God, for it is *not even able* to do so, and those who are in the flesh *cannot* please God" (Rom 8:7–8).

Indeed, in his own power man cannot even make a move toward Christ to ask for salvation. He is absolutely unable to make such a spiritual decision. Thus, Jesus says: "no one *can* come to Me unless the Father who sent Me draws him" (John 6:44). And "no one *can* come to Me unless it has been granted him from the Father" (John 6:65; cp. John 6:44).

This is because unregenerate sinners cannot spiritually discern their need of salvation. Jesus warns: "Why do you not understand what I am saying? It is because you *cannot* hear My word" (John 8:43). Paul writes: "this I say, and affirm together with the Lord, that you walk no longer just as the Gentiles also walk, in the futility of their mind, being darkened in their understanding, excluded from the life of God because of the ignorance that is in them, because of the hardness of their heart" (Eph 4: 17–18).

When the disciples hear his teaching along these lines they are perplexed. And Jesus declares man's spiritual inability: "when the disciples heard this, they were very astonished and said, 'Then who can be saved?' And looking at them Jesus said to them, 'With people this is impossible, but with God all things are possible'" (Matt 19:25–26).

So now we see not only that all men are despicable sinners in God's eyes, but also that their corruption renders it impossible for them either to please God or even to seek him. This is fundamentally important to know as we consider *The Truth about Salvation*. For man is in such a predicament, he cannot save himself.

But there is more. There is the final reality of man's standing before God. So we must now consider:

Man's Record

Man's sinfulness does not simply have implications in the horizontal plane of history. That is, it does not affect only his life and social conduct among fellow sinners on earth. As bad as his earthly condition is, it is even worse for him in the vertical plane in that God notes man's sin in heaven above.

The sinner may view himself in relatively good terms, sometimes even in glowing terms: "there is a kind who is pure in his own eyes" (Prov 30:12a). As Jesus warns: "You are those who justify yourselves in the sight of men, but God knows your hearts; for that which is highly esteemed among men is detestable in the sight of God" (Luke 16:15).

Man may proudly say that he is not a swindler or an adulterer (Luke 18:11). He may even proclaim: "I am not defiled" (Jer 2:23) or "I am innocent" (Jer 2:35). Though he may claim his innocence before earthly associates he cannot do so before his heavenly Judge. The Bible is abundantly clear on this important point:

The God of Scripture is perfect and all-knowing so that no sin escapes his notice.

- "The eyes of the LORD are in every place, / Watching the evil and the good." (Prov 15:3)
- "The eyes of the LORD move to and fro throughout the earth." (2 Chron 16:9)
- "Does He not see my ways / And number all my steps?" (Job 31:4)
- "You have placed our iniquities before You, / Our secret sins in the light of Your presence." (Psa 90:8)
- "For the ways of a man are before the eyes of the LORD, / And He watches all his paths." (Prov 5:21)

"My eyes are on all their ways; they are not hidden from My face, nor is their iniquity concealed from My eyes." (Jer 16:17)

"There is no creature hidden from His sight, but all things are open and laid bare to the eyes of Him with whom we have to do." (Heb 4:13)

In fact, as we read in Job: "What is man, that he should be pure, / Or he who is born of a woman, that he should be righteous?" (Job 15:14). Solomon challenges the world: "Who can say, 'I have cleansed my heart, I am pure from my sin?'" (Prov 20:9). Therefore, the Apostle John warns: "if we say that we have no sin, we are deceiving ourselves and the truth is not in us. . . . If we say that we have not sinned, we make Him a liar and His word is not in us" (1 John 1:8, 10).

As a result of all of this all men have a bad record with God who notes all of their words, thoughts, and deeds: "we know that whatever the Law says, it speaks to those who are under the Law, so that every mouth may be closed and all the world may become accountable to God" (Rom 3:19).

Conclusion

In this portion of our study on salvation we have seen that God's Word teaches us that God created a perfect world, but that Adam rebelled against him. And Adam did so as our representative, so that all men have fallen in him.[5] Adam is the progenitor of the whole human race (even including Eve, Gen 2:21–23) and stood for us in the Garden.

We noted also that what the Bible teaches about man's depravity: it permeates every part of his being and all of his activities. And it does so from the moment of his conception. But not only is he inherently depraved, but because of that depravity he is totally unable to do anything that pleases God. He is even wholly unable to come to Christ for his help because of the blindness of his heart.

Consequently, man has a foul record with God who sees all things and takes note of them. No man can escape accountability before God.

---

[5] We should certainly not complain about our being declared sinners in Adam because we did not personally fail in Eden. After all, on this complaint we would have to deny Christ's righteousness being applied to our accounts because we did not die on the cross at Golgotha.

But there is more. And we shall reflect on this in the next chapter. Man's predicament is exacerbated because he must stand before a perfectly righteous God to give an account of himself.

REVIEW QUESTIONS FOR DISCUSSION

These questions deal directly with the material in this chapter. The answers can be found in the chapter.

1. What are some basic facts that we learn in the creation account of man? How will these impact our understanding of the seriousness of Adam's fall?
2. What is Satan attempting to do in his approaching Eve with his question?
3. Discuss Adam acting as our representative in Eden.
4. How early in each individual's existence in the world does he become a fallen sinner? Provide biblical documentation.
5. Total depravity is a biblical but misunderstood theological concept. What is *not* meant when we speak of "total depravity"?
6. What *do* we mean by "total depravity"?
7. Discuss the concept of man's "total inability." How is this important to better understanding the biblical doctrine of salvation?
8. What are some key verses teaching man's inability before God?
9. Paul is generally viewed as the one who teaches most about man's depravity. Where does Jesus speak about this fundamental problem in man?
10. Discuss man's depravity regarding his relationship to other men. To God.

STRETCHING FURTHER

These questions are designed to promote further group reflection on the topic beyond that which is presented in the chapter above.

1. Before man's fall did animals die? Or was Adam's fall the beginning of the death of sentient life in the world?
2. How is God's testing Adam as our representative fair and for our good?

3. Does man's depravity affect his reasoning process? Cite biblical evidence for your answer.
4. Most men believe they are not as bad as Scripture presents. How does this self-evaluation underscore the fact of their total depravity?
5. What are some reasons that the doctrine of total depravity is so hated by the non-Christian?

Chapter 3
GOD IS A RIGHTEOUS JUDGE

As we saw in our last chapter, man is a miserable sinner. He is a fallen creature and is corrupted by sin in every part of his being. As a result he is even wholly unable to pick himself up so that he might approach God to seek his help. Theologically speaking, in the eyes of God man is totally depraved and therefore totally unable to please him.

But it gets worse.

All of this is terrifyingly significant . . . for God is man's Judge. And unlike human judges, he is absolutely pure and wholly perfect in all of his being and his actions. The sinner needs be warned about the holy character and righteous ways of God if he is to have any hope of eternal salvation. He desperately needs this information so that he might understand *The Truth about Salvation*.

God Is Righteous

Having analyzed man's corrupted character and fallen status, we must now consider his Creator before whom he stands. We must do so in order to put man's dire predicament into proper perspective. His circumstances are alarming because Scripture teaches God's absolute moral perfection. As the Apostle John puts it: "God is Light, and in Him there is no darkness at all" (1 John 1:5b).

God is absolutely righteous. His righteousness involves his strict and unwavering adherence to moral perfection. God's righteousness is his inherent moral purity which is absolute, fixed, and certain: in no way is it relative, arbitrary, or changing. Indeed, Psalm 119:142 states that "Your righteousness is an everlasting righteousness."

God's righteousness is the ultimate standard for righteousness. His perfect righteousness; it is not measured by a standard outside of himself. There is no criterion to which he himself is subject or to which he must submit. Rather, God's moral character *is* that standard for righteousness. Consequently, God declares: "I, the LORD, speak righteousness, / Declaring things that are upright" (Isa 45:19). "It is I who speak in righteousness" (Isa 63:1). In fact, he delights in his own righteousness: "I am the LORD who exercises lovingkindness, justice and righteousness on earth; for I delight in these things" (Jer 9:24).

Because of the absolute perfection of God's being, he is wholly pure and righteous in himself. The Psalmist states that "no evil dwells with You" (Psa 5:4), that "there is no unrighteousness in Him" (Psa 92:15). The Song of Moses proclaims: "The Rock! His work is perfect, / For all His ways are just; / A God of faithfulness and without injustice, / Righteous and upright is He" (Deut 32:4). Therefore, Paul declares: "there is no injustice with God" (Rom 9:14). Thus, "good and upright is the LORD" (Psa 25:8).

So important is this affirmation of God's character that Scripture repeatedly declares it: Ezra 9:15; Nehemiah 9:8; Psalm 119:137; 145:17; Jeremiah 12:1; Lamentation 1:18; Daniel 9:14; John 17:25; 2 Timothy 4:8; 1 John 2:29; 3:7; Revelation 16:5. In fact, the Psalmist strains to portray the absoluteness of God's moral rectitude. "Your righteousness is like the mountains of God" (Psa 36:6). "Your righteousness, O God, reaches to the heavens" (Psa 71:19).

The God before whom men live, is not a god made in the image of man. He is not one who has a relative, imperfect righteousness which makes him roughly equal to men. Rather, God is perfectly righteous and his character is the very standard of righteousness before which men must bow. To lead men to *The Truth about Salvation* they need to know the righteousness of the God who saves.

But there is more, for:

God Is Just

In both the Hebrew of the Old Testament and the Greek of the New Testament one important word-group can be translated in two ways: as "righteous" and as "just." But we can distinguish the two concepts embodied in the word. And this is significant for our present purposes, as we will see.

In the immediately preceding section above, we noted that God is righteous in himself. We will now consider that, as a consequence of his own intrinsic righteousness within, he acts justly (righteously) toward others without. That is, he treats others in terms of his own perfect righteousness. As Paul rhetorically asks: "there is no injustice with God, is there? May it never be!" (Rom 9:14).

Regarding moral issues, man sees in grays, whereas God sees all in black and white (John's writings show this most clearly in his juxtaposing light/dark, good/evil, life/death, love/hate, etc.). Therefore, man tends to assume God will be lenient when it comes to sin. He oftentimes will claim "I am not so bad" or "God will surely accept the good I have done, despite my failures." But as asked in Job 4:17: "Can mankind be just before God? / Can a man be pure before his Maker?" And as Jesus warns in his Sermon on the Mount: "I say to you that unless your righteousness surpasses that of the scribes and Pharisees, you will not enter the kingdom of heaven" (Matt 5:20).

Contrary to man's moral blindness, God's righteousness is perfect. It necessarily obliges him to punish unrighteousness through the exercise of his justice. His righteousness comes to expression in his justice which punishes sin in order to maintain that which is right. Therefore, in the Psalms we read: "Righteous are You, O LORD, / And upright are Your judgments" (Psa 119:137).

In light of God's justice the psalmist warns: "the LORD is in His holy temple; the LORD's throne is in heaven; / His eyes behold, His eyelids test the sons of men" (Psa 11:4). The prophet Habakkuk recognizes of God: "Your eyes are too pure to approve evil, / And You cannot look on wickedness with favor" (Hab 1:13). Thus, God himself declares to Moses that he "will by no means leave the guilty unpunished" (Exo 34:7b; cp. Exo 23:7; Nah 1:3).

As we discuss *The Truth about Salvation* it is vitally important that fallen man be confronted with the absoluteness of his moral failure in the eyes of God. This is because of his looming judgment under God's perfect justice. In Job 13:9 we are warned: "Will it be well when He examines you? / Or will you deceive Him as one deceives a man?" The obvious answer is certainly: "No!" In fact, the Scriptures warn sinners: "Do not be deceived, God is not mocked; for whatever a man sows, this he will also reap" (Gal 6:7).

And this leads us to note that, not only is God intrinsically righteous, and not only is he moved to judge unrighteousness, but in fact:

God Will Judge

As a righteous and just Judge, God must deal with people according to what they deserve according to their moral character and conduct. Consequently, he not only is intrinsically right in himself and just toward others, but he administers his kingdom (the world) according to his own perfect righteousness. That is, his personal righteousness leads to his official righteousness.

The Bible is very clear on the fact that God will judge. After all, "God is a righteous judge, / And a God who has indignation every day" (Psa 7:11). Thus, "He will judge the world in righteousness; / He will execute judgment for the peoples with equity" (Psa 9:8).

The Lord repeatedly warns in Scripture — in *both* testaments — that "vengeance is Mine, and retribution" (Deut 32:35; cp. Psa 94:1; Isa 35:4; Nah 1:2; Rom 12:19; Heb 10:30). Because of this we must warn the sinner that "it is a terrifying thing to fall into the hands of the living God" (Heb 10:31). As Nahum asks: "Who can stand before His indignation? / Who can endure the burning of His anger? / His wrath is poured out like fire / And the rocks are broken up by Him" (Nah 1:6).

Though it may seem for the moment that sinners escape God's judgment, Paul teaches that "He has fixed a day in which He will judge the world in righteousness through a Man whom He has appointed, having furnished proof to all men by raising Him from the dead" (Acts 17:31). He repeats this warning in Romans: "Because of your stubbornness and unrepentant heart you are storing up wrath for yourself in the day of wrath and revelation of the righteous judgment of God, who will render to each person according to his deeds" (Rom 2:5–6).

John provides much detail on Judgment Day and its eternal consequences in Revelation:

> "Then I saw a great white throne and Him who sat upon it, from whose presence earth and heaven fled away, and no place was found for them. And I saw the dead, the great and the small, standing before the throne, and books were opened; and another book was opened, which is the book of life; and the dead were judged from the things which were written in the books, according to their deeds. And the sea gave up the dead which were in it, and death and Hades gave up the dead which were in them; and they were judged, every one of them according to their deeds. Then death and Hades were thrown into the lake of fire. This is the second death, the lake of fire. And if anyone's name was not found written in the book of life, he was thrown into the lake of fire." (Rev 20:11–15)

God Will Judge Eternally

God's wrath on Judgment Day is not just a passing terror, over with and done in a moment. Indeed, the most terrifying prospect of God's judgment is that it continues forever. Judgment Day results in *eternal* damnation, and not in terms of permanent annihilation but in eternal conscious punishment. Since man has an immortal soul and sins against an eternal God, breaking his eternal law, his punishment is eternal.

Though the doctrine of hell is rejected by many evangelical Christians, it is taught throughout Scripture. The Lord Jesus himself teaches more on this doctrine than anyone else. We can see this in a few sample texts.

Jesus teaches that hell involves eternal punishment, for on Judgment Day he will pronounce: "Depart from Me, accursed ones, into the eternal fire which has been prepared for the devil and his angels" (Matt 25:41). He adds: "These will go away into eternal punishment" (Matt 25:46). Thus, he calls the fire of hell "the unquenchable fire" (Mark 9:43), where "their worm does not die, and the fire is not quenched" (Mark 9:48).

Paul agrees when he states that on Judgment Day "the Lord Jesus will be revealed from heaven with His mighty angels in flaming fire, dealing out retribution to those who do not know God and to those who do not obey the gospel of our Lord Jesus. These will pay the penalty of eternal destruction, away from the presence of the Lord and from the glory of His power" (1 Thess 1:7–9).

Christ even teaches that men will suffer in hell after their resurrection and in their eternal, material bodies: "Do not fear those who kill the body but are unable to kill the soul; but rather fear Him who is able to destroy both soul and body in hell" (Matt 10:28; cp. Matt 5:30). See also Matthew 5:22, 29; 7:13. The "destruction" Jesus mentions in Matthew 10:28 does not imply the dissolution of the body, but the destruction of all the comfort, hopes, and dreams of bodily life.

Hell involves *conscious* torment, for in his parable of the Rich Man and Lazarus Jesus presents the rich man as pleading: "send Lazarus so that he may dip the tip of his finger in water and cool off my tongue, for I am in agony in this flame" (Luke 16:24). And the rich man speaks of hell as "this place of torment" (Luke 16:28). Revelation 14:11 pictures the torment of the beast's worshipers similarly: "the smoke of their torment goes up forever and ever; they have no rest day and night, those who worship the beast and his image, and whoever receives the mark of his name."

Conclusion

Man desperately needs to know *The Truth about Salvation* for a variety of reasons. Foremost among those reasons are those that have to do with who God is.

Man does not have to fear standing before other fallen creatures to give an account of his life. He must stand before a righteous God who is perfect in his whole being and in all his ways. Not only so but God's perfect righteousness in himself demands his absolute justice in dealing with others. God will judge all men in his maintaining the integrity of his kingdom.

Not only so, but the most terrifying doctrine of Scripture teaches that the infinitely righteous God will execute his perfect justice eternally. Man's time spent on earth is not the totality of his existence. He is created as immortal creature reflecting (on the creaturely level) the ongoing existence of God who has imposed an eternal law upon him. Therefore, man enters into the afterlife as a sinner who continually deserves God's wrath.

We must warn sinners that "it is a terrifying thing to fall into the hands of the living God" (Heb 10:31). As Paul puts it: "knowing the fear of the Lord, we persuade men" (2 Cor 5:11).

REVIEW QUESTIONS FOR DISCUSSION

These questions deal directly with the material in this chapter. The answers can be found in the chapter.

1. How does God's being our Judge differ from our experience with man's judgment? How is this significant for understanding the necessity of the doctrine of salvation.
2. By what standard do we evaluate God's righteousness? Explain your answer.
3. Discuss how man views moral behavior differently from God.
4. How much unrighteousness can God tolerate? Provide Bible evidence for your answer.
5. Why is it important in presenting salvation to others that we emphasize God's perspective on man's moral behavior?
6. Discuss the distinction between God's personal righteousness and his official righteousness.

7. Scripture teaches that God judges unrighteousness. But we see so much unrighteousness continuing on in the world. How can we explain this?
8. List some biblical evidence for God's eternal judgment of men in hell.
9. Do the lost suffer in hell only in their spirits? Provide biblical evidence for your answer.
10. How is the doctrine of hell to encourage our desire to proclaim the gospel?

STRETCHING FURTHER

These questions are designed to promote further group reflection on the topic beyond that which is presented in the chapter above.

1. Discuss the meaning and significance of the statement by the French Enlightenment philosopher Voltaire (1694–1778[1]): "If God has made us in his image, we have returned him the favor."
2. Since Jesus command: "Do not judge so that you will not be judged" (Matt 7:1), how is it that Christians may rightly judge sinful behavior in others? Explain what Jesus means.
3. The Bible teaches that the lost enter into hell at their death. But it also teaches that God will resurrect them and judge them on Judgment Day. How can both of these perspectives be right?
4. How can God justly punish a sinner eternally who only lived for fifty, sixty, or seventy years on earth?
5. List some alternative views proposed by Christians in the place of the doctrine of eternal hell.

---

[1] "Voltaire" is his pen name. His real name was François-Marie Arouet.

Chapter 4
GOD IS A GRACIOUS REDEEMER

Given man's total depravity and God's absolute righteousness, we might despairingly wonder: "How then can a man be just with God?" (Job 25:4; cp. Job 9:2). And this is the most important question a man can ponder.

In fact, the disciples hear Jesus declare the difficulty of salvation even for the law-abiding rich man: he likens the difficulty to a camel going through the eye of a needle (Luke 17:24–25). They respond to him in surprise and alarm: "then who can be saved?" (Luke 17:26). But Jesus replies: "The things that are impossible with people are possible with God" (Luke 18:27). And the reason is: because God is a gracious Redeemer.

The Definition of Redemptive Grace

The word "grace" in the Bible is not always used as a redemptive term. In fact, neither does it always bear the same basic meaning (e.g., it can mean attractive, gift, or thanks).

Nevertheless, the most important idea involved in grace in its most widely used meaning speaks of an active favor or good will extended from one person to another, whether from God to man (Gen 6:8; Exo 34:9) or from man to man (Gen 33:15; 1 Sam 1:18). Fundamental to this meaning of grace is that it involves a *benefit* that is *freely given* in *kindness* to another who has *no claim* on the giver.

We find a general use of the term "grace" that clearly exhibits this significance in Lot's experience. Genesis uses the Hebrew for "grace" in Lot's response to one of the angels who come to escort him to safety before God destroys Sodom (Gen 19:15–17). In Genesis 19:19 we read of Lot's thankful recognition of the angel's display of grace: "Now behold, your servant has found *favor* in your sight, and you have magnified your lovingkindness, which you have shown me by saving my life."

But the grace in which we are interested is the grace of God in salvation. The general idea of grace is gloriously magnified in his specific saving mercy in behalf of the sinner.

God's redemptive grace is his unmerited work in behalf of sinners, by which they receive the benefit of forgiveness of sin and eternal salvation from God's judgment.

Indeed, as theologian Louis Berkhof explains: "grace is an attribute of God, one of the divine perfections. It is God's free, sovereign, undeserved favour or love to man, in his state of sin and guilt, which manifests itself in the forgiveness of sin and deliverance from its penalty."[1]

Because of man's sin (see ch 2) he deserves God's wrath (see ch 3), yet because of God's grace he receives God's blessing. As Peter expresses it to his audience: God saves man from his sin because he is "the God of all grace, who has called you to His eternal glory in Christ" (1 Pet 5:10). In salvation Christ, the Son of God, stands in for the sinner and endures God's righteous judgment upon sin, so that the sinner himself may be saved. This is why God turns his face from Christ as he suffers on the cross (Matt 27:46).

For instance, in 2 Corinthians 5:21 we read that God "made Him who knew no sin to be sin on our behalf, so that we might become the righteousness of God in Him." Paul teaches us that Christ "was delivered over because of our transgressions" (Rom 4:25; cp. Rom 8:32; Gal 2:20; Eph 5:2). Indeed, he states that "Christ redeemed us from the curse of the Law, having become a curse for us" (Gal 3:13).

But there is more.

God's saving grace is not only granted to the *un*deserving but to the *ill*-deserving. That is, we should not illustrate God's grace in salvation as being like someone giving a gift to a homeless person, i.e., the undeserving. Rather it is better to picture it as someone giving a gift to a homeless person *after the homeless person has viciously attacked him*, i.e., to the ill-deserving. Grace is undeserved favor for the ill-deserving sinner.

So then, as we should understand from our earlier study of sin, we are sinners who deserve the opposite of God's favor: we deserve his wrath. For "God demonstrates His own love toward us, in that *while we were yet sinners*, Christ died for us" (Rom 5:8). Indeed, Christ "died for the ungodly" (Rom 5:6). Because of its theological usage, the English word "grace" has served as a useful acronym for God's saving love for sinners: God's Riches At Christ's Expense.

---

[1] Louis Berkhof, *Systematic Theology* (Grand Rapids: Eerdmans, 1938), 427.

As a consequence of God's saving grace, Paul can write that "having been justified by faith, we have peace with God through our Lord Jesus Christ, through whom also we have obtained our introduction by faith into this grace in which we stand; and we exult in hope of the glory of God" (Rom 5:1–2). Thus, simply put, the "gospel" (literally: "good news") is "the gospel of the grace of God" (Acts 20:24). We truly "receive the abundance of grace and of the gift of righteousness . . . through the One, Jesus Christ" (Rom 5:17).

But now let us consider:

The Beginning of Redemptive Grace

To better understand the glory of God as a gracious Redeemer, we must once again look back to the beginning. For immediately upon Adam's fall into sin (bringing corruption into man's being and ruin into his history), God promises redemption. Thus, God dramatically exhibits his grace by exercising it in the very historical context of man's rebellion.

Even as God calls down his curse upon Satan, Adam, and Eve, he promises a coming Redeemer for man. In Genesis 3:15 we read God's curse upon Satan which simultaneously presents his blessing upon man: "I will put enmity Between you and the woman, / And between your seed and her seed; / He shall bruise you on the head, / And you shall bruise him on the heel." In these words we may discern several important truths.

First, we see that because of his sin and the enmity of Satan, man must expect conflict in history. This brief prophecy presents us with a mighty, history-long struggle between the serpent's seed and the woman's seed. The tranquility in Eden has been breached and the turbulence in history has begun. We see the immediate results of this conflict in Eve's firstborn son, Cain, killing her second son, Abel (Gen 4:1–8). This murderous hostility continues as we see in Lamech (Gen 4:23–24), in Noah's day (Gen 6:5), and throughout Scripture. It becomes so bad that God says "I will blot out man whom I have created . . , for I am sorry that I have made them" (Gen 6:7).

But, second, we see that God presents two seed lines that will engage the struggle in history. The word for "seed" here "can refer to an immediate descendant (Gen. 4:25; 15:3), a distant offspring [Gal 3:16, 19], or a rather large group of descendants [Gen 22:17; Psa 105:6]. Here and throughout Scripture, all three senses are developed and merged in tracing this concept. In our Genesis text we can infer both the single and collective senses."[2]

The two seed lines which are traced throughout Scripture are the seed of the serpent and the seed of the woman. The seed of the serpent is not a literal lineage, but a spiritual line of people who follow Satan's original rebellion against God: this line includes all the non-elect (Matt 13:38; John 8:44). The seed of the woman involves both a literal singular seed (Christ) and a spiritual corporate seed which follows God's original intention for Eve: they are the elect (John 1:12; 11:52; 1 John 3:1–2).

After Cain slays Abel we read of the birth of Seth's son, Enosh. There we discover that "then men began to call upon the name of the LORD" (Gen 4:26). John presents these antithetical seed lines as "the children of God and the children of the devil" (1 John 3:8, cp. Matt 13:48; John 8:44; 1 John 3:10).

The ultimate individual, literal seed of the woman is Jesus Christ, the Redeemer of God's elect. "When the fullness of the time came, God sent forth His Son, born of a woman, born under the Law, so that He might redeem those who were under the Law, that we might receive the adoption as sons " (Gal 4:4–5). Luke traces Jesus' genealogy from Mary back to "the son of Enosh, the son of Seth, the son of Adam, the son of God" (Luke 3:38).

Third, the seed of the woman (Christ) will conquer the seed of the serpent (Satan). Though Satan will bruise his heel (a painful wound), Christ will crush his head (a mortal blow). Despite Satan's attempt to corrupt mankind and destroy God's work, God here promises to send a Redeemer who will conquer him by means of his redemptive grace. God's seed will secure victory in history.[3]

Thus, the prophecy in Genesis 3:15 is theologically called the "protoevangelium," the first promise ("proto") of the gospel ("evangelium") and its victory in history. In fact, it is the first prophecy in Scripture and it points to the coming of our Redeemer, Jesus Christ the Son of God in whom he is well-pleased (Matt 3:16; 17:5). God is indeed a gracious Redeemer.

---

[2] Bruce K. Waltke, *Genesis: A Commentary* (Grand Rapids: Zondervan, 2001), 93.

[3] See another book in the *Truth About* series: Kenneth L. Gentry, Jr., *The Truth about Postmillennialism* (Chesnee, SC: Victorious Hope, 2019).

The Expansion of Redemptive Grace

God's grace begins in the Garden where the fall occurs, but flows out from there into the broader world. By Noah's time, however, it seems that the seed of the serpent will win the struggle, for "the wickedness of man was great on the earth . . . and every intent of the thoughts of his heart was only evil continually" (Gen 6:5). But God's grace is stronger than Satan's graft, for "Noah found favor [grace] in the eyes of the LORD" (Gen 6:8).

God graciously establishes his covenant with Noah to rebuild the human race. "Behold, I, even I am bringing the flood of water upon the earth, to destroy all flesh in which is the breath of life, from under heaven; everything that is on the earth shall perish. But I will establish My covenant with you; and you shall enter the ark — you and your sons and your wife, and your sons' wives with you" (Gen 6:17–18; cp. 1 Pet 3:20; 2 Pet 2:5).

Following the seed of the woman through her son Seth (Gen 4:25; 5:6) on through Noah (Gen 5:29; 10:1) and on further through Shem (Gen 11:10), we finally come to Abram (Gen 11:27). Here we discover God's gracious covenant with Abram/Abraham. The Abrahamic Covenant is a major redemptive divine covenant. In fact, it is foundational to redemption and the messianic hope, as we see from the New Testament repeatedly mentioning it (e.g., Luke 1:55, 73; Acts 3:25; Rom 4:12–16; Gal 3:6–18).

The core of the Abrahamic Covenant appears in Genesis 12:2–3 (cp. Gen 15:5–7), which records God's pre-covenantal promise:

"I will make you a great nation, / And I will bless you, / And make your name great; / And so you shall be a blessing; / And I will bless those who bless you, / And the one who curses you I will curse. / And in you all the families of the earth shall be blessed."

This glorious covenant has enormous implications for the victory of the seed of the woman. It powerfully declares that "*all the families of the earth shall be blessed*" through Abraham. In fact, through it we as Gentile Christians become heirs of Abraham: "If you belong to Christ, then you are Abraham's offspring, heirs according to promise" (Gal 3:29; cp. Rom 4:12–13, 16; Gal 3:7–9, 14).

Thus, the goal of God's redemptive promise in Genesis 3:15 ultimately will include "all the families of the earth." So then, the ultimate purpose of this covenant is nothing less than worldwide salvation. This is why Paul can say that the gospel "is the power of God for salvation to everyone who believes, to the Jew first and also to the Greek" (Rom 1:16).

Paul explains that "the Scripture, foreseeing that God would justify the *Gentiles* by faith, preached the *gospel* beforehand to Abraham, saying, '*All the nations* shall be blessed in you'" (Gal 3:8). Elsewhere he emphasizes the global glory of the Abrahamic Covenant, when he declares that "the promise" to Abraham is that "he would be heir of the *world*" (Rom 4:13).

The seed of the woman will powerfully crush the seed of the serpent. And that will be by God's redemptive grace in Christ. When you challenge sinners with the gospel, you must remember the power of God's grace to save.

The Sovereignty of Redemptive Grace

Before we conclude this chapter, we must recognize a powerful biblical truth regarding God's redemptive grace: its eternal and sovereign nature.

The reason we can read of the sure prophecy of the victory of the woman's seed in Genesis 3:15 is because it is assured by God's eternal, sovereign, elective purpose. This is also the reason why we can confidently present the gospel to rebellious sinners: God saves sinners; we do not. Though the particular individual we seek to evangelize may never be converted, Christians may confidently believe that God will save all those whom he wills to save. We deliver the message; God secures the results.

Paul powerfully teaches the doctrine of God's sovereignty in salvation: God "*chose* us in Him *before* the foundation of the world, that we would be holy and blameless before Him. In love He *predestined* us to adoption as sons through Jesus Christ to Himself, *according to the kind intention of His will*. . . . Also we have obtained an inheritance, having been *predestined* according to His purpose who *works all things* after the counsel of His will" (Eph 1:4–5, 11).

Ephesians 1 contains the key passage for presenting God's absolute sovereignty in salvation. These verses declare both that God "chose us" and that "he predestined us." It also locates when he chose and predestined us: "before the foundation of the world." It declares God's sovereignty to be an aspect of his "love" and an expression of his "kind intention" (i.e., grace), which are rooted in "his will." Later in Ephesians

Paul speaks of "the eternal purpose which He carried out in Christ Jesus our Lord" (Eph 3:11–12).

Paul provides us more insights into God's sovereign, eternal grace in one of his pastoral epistles. In 2 Timothy 1:9 he states that God "has saved us and called us with a holy calling, not according to our works, but according to His *own purpose* and *grace* which was granted us in Christ Jesus *from all eternity*." This passage is almost as powerful as that in Ephesians 1. Here Paul is clearly speaking of salvation when he says "he has saved us." He sees salvation as resulting from the "holy calling" of God. And he makes sure that we do not believe that *any* aspect of salvation results from our own effort, for he states that it is "not according to our works." Salvation is 100% determined "according to his own purpose and grace," and that "from all eternity."

We can see the historical repercussions of God's eternal election in various places in the New Testament (e.g., Matt 13:13–17; John 3:8; 6:37; Acts 18:10; 2 Thess 2:13–14; Rev 13:8). I will focus on just one. Luke reports that "when the Gentiles heard this, they began rejoicing and glorifying the word of the Lord; and as many as had been appointed to eternal life believed" (Acts 13:48). Here Luke is reporting on Paul's gospel preaching (Acts 13:46–47). He notes that the Gentiles are joyfully receiving the good news of salvation, even though the Jews are rejecting it. He points out that "many" Gentiles "believed."

Paul even goes further and theologically explains *why* these Gentiles believe. They believe because they "had been appointed to eternal life." Indeed, he notes that only "as many as had been appointed to eternal life" actually respond in faith. Why did these respond, and not others? Because that is how many God had "appointed to eternal life." As Jesus teaches earlier: even though "no one can come to Me unless the Father who sent Me draws him" (John 6:44), nevertheless "all that the Father gives Me will come to Me" (John 6:37). [4]

Conclusion

In order to properly grasp *The Truth about Salvation*, we need to recognize man's desperate condition. We must understand that though man is created by God and in his image (ch 1). And yet he is a sinner who is

---

[4] For more on God's absolute sovereignty, see: Kenneth L. Gentry, Jr., *Predestination Made Easy* (Chesnee, SC: Victorious Hope, 2010).

totally depraved (in all parts of his being) and therefore unable even to come to God for salvation (see ch 2). We must also recognize that he lives under the righteous condemnation of God (ch 3).

Nevertheless, we may take heart in God's grace which he initiates immediately upon man's sin in establishing a gracious seed line (Gen 3:15). Even while man is in his most vigorous state of rebellion in Noah's day (Gen 6:5–7), God's grace intervenes to insure the spiritual seed line continues (Gen 6:8, 18). Not only so, but he promises that it will expand to "all the families of the earth" (Gen 12:3).

God chooses us from before the foundation of the world (Eph 1:4) and calls us with "a holy calling" (1 Tim 1:9). He sovereignly opens the heart of the lost when it is his will to do so. We may see this clearly stated in Lydia's case: she "was listening; and the Lord opened her heart to respond to the things spoken by Paul" (Acts 16:14). Consequently, she is evidence that God appoints many to eternal life by his sovereign grace.

REVIEW QUESTIONS FOR DISCUSSION

These questions deal directly with the material in this chapter. The answers can be found in the chapter.

1. What is the most important question men must consider? Why?
2. Does "grace" in the original languages of Scripture always speak of God's redemptive grace? Explain what the basic word means in itself.
3. What is a good definition of redemptive grace?
4. Why does God turn his face from Christ when he dies on the cross?
5. Discuss the difference between saying man is "undeserving" and saying he is "ill-deserving."
6. What does the word "gospel" mean in the original language of Scripture? How does this capture the significance of God's grace?
7. When do we first see in Scripture God's grace arising despite man's sin?
8. Who is the ultimate "seed of the woman"? What biblical evidence can you provide for your answer?
9. Is God's grace merited by man? Or sovereignly granted by God? What are some Bible verses supporting your answer?
10. Discuss the significance of Acts 13:48 regarding salvation.

STRETCHING FURTHER

These questions are designed to promote further group reflection on the topic beyond that which is presented in the chapter above.

1. Do you think Adam was redeemed and is in heaven? Why?
2. Discuss Genesis 3:15 and its theological meaning regarding salvation.
3. Since not all men will be saved, what does Scripture mean when the Abrahamic Covenant states: "in you all the families of the earth shall be blessed"?
4. If Christ defeats Satan at the cross, how can we explain Satan's continuing evil work?
5. What does Scripture mean by "predestination"?

Chapter 5
JESUS IS A DIVINE SAVIOR

We are called "Christians" (Acts 11:26) and are committed to the "Christian" faith (Acts 26:28; 1 Pet 4:16). Consequently, Christ is central to our doctrine and practice. Indeed, he is not only central to Christianity, he is absolutely essential to it. And as such he is fundamental to explaining *The Truth about Salvation*.

As we begin a two-chapter study of Christ as Savior we must first recognize that:

Man Needs a Perfect Savior

As we saw in earlier chapters, man is wholly corrupted by sin. As Isaiah poetically pictures Israel's condition, so may we characterize mankind's condition before God: "the whole head is sick / And the whole heart is faint / From the sole of the foot even to the head / There is nothing sound in it, / Only bruises, welts and raw wounds" (Isa 1:5–6).

Indeed, David observes that "in Your sight no man living is righteous" (Psa 143:2). He states this because "there is no man who does not sin" (1 Kgs 8:46; cp. Eccl 7:20; Rom 3:10, 20). Yet as an immortal creature made in God's image (Gen 1:26), he desperately needs salvation. He must have his positive relationship with his Creator restored, for as we read in Ecclesiastes: "God made men upright, but they have sought out many devices" (Eccl 7:29).

On his own merit and by his own strength it is impossible for man to secure his salvation. This is because God is an absolutely perfect God and cannot accept imperfection. As Habakkuk confesses to God: "Your eyes are too pure to approve evil, / And you cannot look on wickedness with favor" (Hab 1:13). The Psalmist asks: "if You, LORD, should mark iniquities, O Lord, who could stand?" (Psa 130:3). Consequently, Eliphaz asks: "Can mankind be just before God? / Can a man be pure before his Maker?" (Job 4:17; cp. Job 9:2; 25:4).

God is holy and perfect and therefore morally separate from sinful men. Moses praises God by rhetorically asking: "Who is like You among the gods, O LORD? / Who is like You, majestic in holiness?" (Exo 15:11).

Indeed, God himself declares: My "name is Holy, / I dwell on a high and holy place" (Isa 57:15), meaning he is absolutely holy in his being and majestically exalted in righteousness high above man.

Not only has man's sin broken his relationship with his Creator, but he is in a state of enmity (Rom 5:10) against God and alienation from him (Col 1:21; cp. Eph 2:12). He has not only failed to please God and meet God's requirements, but his nature is so corrupt that he "cannot please God" (Rom 8:8).

Because of God's holiness and man's sinfulness, man needs a perfect Savior. And because of his marvelous grace we may rejoice that:

God Effects a Salvation Plan

In the preceding chapter we saw how God sovereignly saves sinners by means of his eternal grace in election and predestination (Eph 1:4, 11). We saw also that he establishes his gracious covenant with his elect people (Gen 12:2–3; Jer 31:31–34). At this point in our study we need to consider what theologians call "the covenant of redemption," which is the eternal source of the historical covenant of grace.

The covenant of redemption is not a covenant between God and man, rather it is an intra-Trinitarian covenant between the members of the Godhead. That is, it is a pre-temporal agreement between God the Father, God the Son, and God the Holy Spirit wherein each Person of the Trinity commits to particular actions necessary for securing the salvation of the elect. Though the Scriptures do not expressly speak of a "covenant of redemption," we can find traces of it therein. Let us see how this is so.

The Bible specifically mentions that the Father agrees to send the Son to redeem the people whom he elects for salvation. And that the Son agrees to accomplish that task by suffering and dying for their sins. Jesus frequently speaks of his Father's *sending* him to accomplish the eternal plan of redemption. We see this most clearly in his high priestly prayer not long before he is crucified:

> "This is eternal life, that they may know You, the only true God, and Jesus Christ whom You have *sent*. I glorified You on the earth, having accomplished *the work* which *You have given Me* to do. Now, Father, glorify Me together with Yourself, with *the glory* which I had with You *before the world was*." (John 17:3–5)

In fact, Jesus informs the Jews who are resisting him: "If God were your Father, you would love Me, for I *proceeded forth* and *have come* from God, for I have not even come on My own initiative, but *He sent Me*" (John 8:42). Indeed, "the Father has sent the Son to be the Savior of the world" (1 Jn 4:14).[1] God's sending of his Son is a recurring theme in John's writings, as we may see in John 3:34; 5:36, 38; 6:29, 38, 57; 7:29; 8:42; 10:36; 11:42; 17:3, 8, 21, 23, 25; 20:21; and 1 John 4:9, 10, 14.

God's sending his own Son is not a unique thought in John's writings, however, for we also read of it in Paul: "What the Law could not do, weak as it was through the flesh, God did: *sending* His own Son in the likeness of sinful flesh and as an offering for sin" (Rom 8:3). Interestingly, Paul even uses the word *apostellō* ("send with a commission") of God's sending the Son to be our Redeemer: "when the fullness of the time came, God *sent forth* His Son, born of a woman, born under the Law, so that He might redeem those who were under the Law, that we might receive the adoption as sons."[2]

The writer of Hebrews puts Old Testament words in the mouth of Jesus in showing that he comes to effect redemption: "I said, 'Behold, I have come (in the scroll of the book it is written of me) to do your will, O God.' after saying above, 'sacrifices and offerings and whole burnt offerings and sacrifices for sin you have not desired, nor have you taken pleasure in them' (which are offered according to the law), then he said, 'Behold, I have come to do your will.' He takes away the first in order to establish the second" (Heb 10:7–9).

As a Trinitarian plan, the covenant of redemption involves the work of the Spirit as well. He empowers Christ to successfully complete his redemptive labor. "Jesus, full of the Holy Spirit, returned from the Jordan and was led around by the Spirit in the wilderness for forty days, being tempted by the devil" (Luke 4:1–2). "For He whom God has sent speaks

---

[1] By his being the Savior of the world, John means that salvation will eventually win the world as system of men and things, i.e., as a whole, rather than simply snatching brands from the fire. This does not imply that each and every individual will be saved, but that the bulk of mankind will one day be saved so that Christianity will become the rule rather than the exception. See my book *The Truth about Postmillennialism* (Chesnee, SC: Victorious Hope, 2019).

[2] Other New Testament statements also record this potent word for sending the Son: Matt 10:40; 15:24; Luke 9:48; 10:16; John 3:17, 34; 5:36, 38; 6:29, 57; 7:29; 8:42; 10:36; 17:3, 8, 18, 21, 23, 25; Acts 3:20, 26; 1 Jn 4:9, 10, 14.

the words of God; for He gives the Spirit [to Christ] without measure" (John 3:34).

The Holy Spirit also sovereignly promotes the Son's saving work in the world. He inspires the Apostles to receive and proclaim the truth: "When the Helper comes, whom I will send to you from the Father, that is the Spirit of truth who proceeds from the Father, He will testify about Me, and you will testify also, because you have been with Me from the beginning" (John 14:26–27; Acts 1:8).

In addition, the Spirit applies salvation to the elect: "Truly, truly, I say to you, unless one is born of water and the Spirit he cannot enter into the kingdom of God. That which is born of the flesh is flesh, and that which is born of the Spirit is spirit. Do not be amazed that I said to you, 'You must be born again.' The wind blows where it wishes and you hear the sound of it, but do not know where it comes from and where it is going; so is everyone who is born of the Spirit" (John 3:5–8). As Paul puts it: "He saved us, not on the basis of deeds which we have done in righteousness, but according to His mercy, by the washing of regeneration and renewing by the Holy Spirit, whom He poured out upon us richly through Jesus Christ our Savior" (Tit 3:5–6).

Jesus is God In the Flesh

So now, since God is a perfect, righteous, and holy God who cannot tolerate sin, how can he save sinners while maintaining his inflexible righteousness? How can he establish his covenant of redemption for saving sinners when they actually deserve his wrath and condemnation? He can do so by sending his perfect Son to stand in as a representative for the sinner.

Biblical Christianity affirms the deity of Christ noting that he is truly and fully God. No understanding of *The Truth about Salvation* can overlook the fact of Jesus' deity for it is necessary for our salvation for at least three reasons:

1. The Redeemer must be of infinite value to pay the debt incurred by the breaking God's eternal law.
2. The Redeemer must be of sufficient value to cover the sins of the great multitude of the elect.

3. The Redeemer must be equal with God so that man might become the obedient servant of God rather than of another.[3]

The Bible is abundantly clear that Jesus Christ is God the Son, the second person of the Trinity. Consider the following lines of evidence.

1. The Bible declares Jesus is God

Perhaps the best known verse stating Jesus' deity is John 1:1: "In the beginning was the Word, and the Word was with God, and the Word was God." A few verses later John informs us that he is speaking of Jesus: "And the Word became flesh, and dwelt among us" (John 1:14). Here we not only see that the one who became flesh "was God," but that he was also "in the beginning" and was "with God."

John 20:28 also applies this label to Christ. When Jesus first appears to the disciples after the resurrection, Thomas is not present with them and refuses to believe he arose from the dead (John 20:24–25). But when Jesus appears to the disciples a second time, Thomas is with them. When the Lord encourages him to believe that he is risen, we read that "Thomas answered and said to Him, 'My Lord and my God!'" (John 20:28). We must note that he is not using the Lord's name in vain. Rather he says this "to Him," calling him "My Lord and my God."

Paul states of Christ Jesus that "He existed in the form of God" though He "did not regard equality with God a thing to be grasped" (Phil 2:6). This statement declares that Jesus exists in the very form of God, meaning that he is everything that God is. That which is the form of a chair is a chair; that which is the form of God is God. Paul also speaks of his "equality with God," even though it declares that he does not seize that truth in order to avoid "death, even death on a cross" (Phil 2:8).

---

[3] Anselm of Canterbury (1033–1109) in his work "Why God Became Man" presents this interesting argument for Christ's deity: "Do you not perceive that, if any other being should rescue man from eternal death, man would rightly be adjudged as the servant of that being? Now if this be so, he would in no wise be restored to that dignity which would have been his had he never sinned. For he, who was to be through eternity only the servant of God and an equal with the holy angels, would now be the servant of a being who was not God, and whom the angels did not serve."

Matching his statement in Philippians 2:6, Paul states in his Epistle to the Colossians: "For in Him all the fullness of Deity dwells in bodily form" (Col 2:9).

We see the "God" used of Christ in other passages as well: Romans 9:5; Titus 2:13; Hebrews 1:8; and 2 Peter 1:1.

2. Jesus claims to be God

Since Jesus is God we should expect that he himself claims to be so. And he does. In John 5:17 Jesus says: "My Father is working until now, and I Myself am working." The Jews understood that he is equating himself with God, for we read: "therefore the Jews were seeking all the more to kill Him, because He not only was breaking the Sabbath, but also was calling God His own Father, making Himself equal with God" (John 5:19).

When he is debating the Jews in John 8 he claims the covenant name of God: "Jesus said to them, 'Truly, truly, I say to you, before Abraham was born, I am'" (John 8:58). In the Old Testament God identifies himself to Moses as "I Am" (Exo 3:14). The Jews understood Jesus' meaning, for we read: "Therefore they picked up stones to throw at Him" (John 8:59).

He declares his oneness with God, to which the Jews respond by attempting to stone him to death: "'I and the Father are one.' The Jews picked up stones again to stone Him. Jesus answered them, 'I showed you many good works from the Father; for which of them are you stoning Me?' The Jews answered Him, 'For a good work we do not stone You, but for blasphemy; and because You, being a man, make Yourself out to be God'" (John 10:30–33).

After three years of ministry with Philip, the Lord rebukes him for not recognizing this: "Have I been so long with you, and yet you have not come to know Me, Philip? He who has seen Me has seen the Father; how can you say, 'Show us the Father'?" (John 14:9).

When he is on trial the high priest asks him: "Are You the Christ, the Son of the Blessed One?' And Jesus said, 'I am'" (Mark 14:61–62). The high priest understands him to be declaring his deity: "Tearing his clothes, the high priest said, 'What further need do we have of witnesses? You have heard the blasphemy; how does it seem to you?' And they all condemned Him to be deserving of death" (Mark 14:63–64).

Since he claims to be God, we should not be surprised that:

3. Jesus is equal with God

We see Jesus deemed as equal to God in several ways. He is worshiped, which he himself declares should be done for God alone: "You shall worship the Lord your God, and serve Him only" (Matt 4:10; cp. John 5:23). When he stills the storm "those who were in the boat worshiped Him, saying, 'You are certainly God's Son!" (Matt 14:33). After his resurrection some of his disciples fell at his feet to worship him, without his rebuking them: "they came up and took hold of His feet and worshiped Him" (Matt 28:9). In fact, Scripture commands his angels to worship him: "when He again brings the firstborn into the world, He says, 'and let all the angels of God worship him'" (Heb 1:6).

His name stands along with God's name in the baptismal formula: "Go therefore and make disciples of all the nations, baptizing them in the name of the Father and the Son and the Holy Spirit" (Matt 28:19). His name stands with God's in spiritual benedictions: "The grace of the Lord Jesus Christ, and the love of God, and the fellowship of the Holy Spirit, be with you all" (1 Cor 13:14; cp. Rom 1:7; 1 Cor 1:3; 2 Cor 1:2; Gal 1:3; Eph 1:2).

His name brings forgiveness of sin: "Repent, and each of you be baptized in the name of Jesus Christ for the forgiveness of your sins" (Acts 2:38), though God alone can forgive sin (Isa 43:25; 55:7). In Matthew 9:6 he presents his power to heal "so that you may know that the Son of Man has authority on earth to forgive sins" (cp. John 8:24). To him belongs "the glory forever and ever" (Heb 13:21).

His actions were such that the Jews quickly recognized that he considered himself equal with God: "for this reason therefore the Jews were seeking all the more to kill Him, because He not only was breaking the Sabbath, but also was calling God His own Father, making Himself equal with God" (John 5:18). "The Jews answered Him, 'For a good work we do not stone You, but for blasphemy; and because You, being a man, make Yourself out to be God'" (John 10:33; cp. John 19:7).

4. Jesus has the attributes of God

The Bible ascribes divine attributes to Christ. We will cite a representative verse for each attribute then list a few additional verse addresses under each attribute. We will not mention all the various attributes presented in Scripture, but an important sampling of the key ones.

Eternality: "I am the Alpha and the Omega, the first and the last, the beginning and the end" (Rev 22:13), which is a description applied to God (Rev 1:8). See also Isaiah 9:6; Micah 5:2; John 1:1–2; 8:58; 17:5, 24.

Omniscience (all-knowing): "He did not need anyone to testify concerning man, for He Himself knew what was in man" (John 2:25). See also: Mark 2:8; John 1:48; 16:30; 18:4; 21:17.

Omnipresence (everywhere present): "For where two or three have gathered together in My name, I am there in their midst" (Matt 18:20). See also: Matthew 28:20; Ephesians 1:23; Colossians 3:11.

Omnipotence (all powerful): "He is before all things, and in Him all things hold together" (Col 1:17). See also: Philippians 3:21; Hebrews 1:3.

5. Jesus performs the works of God

He performs miracles such as multiplying the loaves and fishes (Matt 14:19), stilling the storm (Matt 8:26–27), and turning the water into wine (John 2:1–11). Though God gifts his apostles and prophets with similar powers, Jesus' power is inherent within himself, for when he turns the water to wine we read: "this beginning of His signs Jesus did in Cana of Galilee, and manifested His glory" (John 1:11; cp. Matt 8:27)

He is the creator of the world. "All things came into being through Him, and apart from Him nothing came into being that has come into being" (John 1:3). "He was in the world, and the world was made through Him, and the world did not know Him" (John 1:10). See also: 1 Corinthians 8:6; Colossians 1:16; Hebrews 1:2; Revelation 3:14.

Conclusion

Truly, Jesus Christ is the Son of God who has the worth and merit to stand in for the multitude of God's elect. Some of the leading heresies in Christianity are those denying the full deity of Christ. Many of the ancient creeds speak directly to the true identity of Jesus as God's Son because of its significance for his work.

But more is necessary for Jesus' work as Redeemer. Therefore, in our next chapter we will focus on the fact that Jesus is a human Savior.

REVIEW QUESTIONS FOR DISCUSSION

These questions deal directly with the material in this chapter. The answers can be found in the chapter.

1. How is the deity of Christ significant for the doctrine of salvation?
2. What is the "covenant of redemption"? Provide biblical evidence for this covenant.
3. How is the covenant of redemption related to the covenant of grace?
4. Which Gospel seems to emphasize Christ's deity the most? Cite some references.
5. List three verses that you see as fundamental to the doctrine of Christ's deity.
6. Where does the Bible teach the pre-existence of Christ? How does this impact our understanding of his deity?
7. Discuss the role of each member of the Trinity in the plan of salvation.
8. What are some leading reasons why Christ must be divine in order to save men from their sins?
9. Besides direct statements affirming Christ's deity, what are some other lines of evidence leading to this conclusion?
10. Is there any evidence in the New Testament that non-Christians understood the Christians' claim that Christ was God (whether or not they believed it)? Where do we find such evidence?

STRETCHING FURTHER

These questions are designed to promote further group reflection on the topic beyond that which is presented in the chapter above.

1. What are some religious movements or persons in history who have denied the deity of Christ?
2. Have you ever interacted with someone who claims to be a Christian but who denies Christ's deity?
3. What are some objections that some who claim to be Christians bring against the doctrine of the deity of Christ?
4. Regarding the work of God, how does the plan of salvation fundamentally differ from the plan proposed by non-Christian religions?

5. Discuss how we can hold to doctrinal constructs (such as the "covenant of redemption") when the Bible does not expressly mention them (we do not find the phrase "covenant of redemption" in Scripture).

Chapter 6
JESUS IS A HUMAN SAVIOR

In our last chapter we noted two important truths for salvation: God has a plan of salvation and that plan includes Jesus Christ as God the Son. The deity of Christ is necessary for our salvation. But though his deity is a *necessary* condition of salvation, it is not a *sufficient* condition. That is, we must have a divine Savior but he must *also* be a human Savior.

For a person to be equipped for saving men, he must: (1) have a connection to the human race so that he can stand with man; and (2) be able to suffer the consequences of God's broken law by enduring his holy wrath against sin. A Savior cannot accomplish either work in his divine nature. Consequently, to properly grasp *The Truth about Salvation* we must also consider that: Christ is a human Savior.

One of the early heresies in the Christian church is known as "docetism." This word derives from the Greek verb *dokein* which is a common word that means "to seem, appear, presume, suppose." The noun *dokēsis* means "phantom, apparition, illusion." Though docetism had a variety of branches, the system basically held that Christ only *seemed* to have a human body. Due to their metaphysic (their philosophy of reality), they deemed matter as imperfect and impure. So as a consequence Jesus must have actually been a spirit who only presented himself as if he had a body.

An early form of docetism even appears in New Testament times. John's first epistle opens with a statement against this view: "What was from the beginning, what we have heard, what we have seen with our eyes, what we have looked at and touched with our hands, concerning the Word of Life" (1 John 1:1). In fact, towards the end of his letter John warns about this movement:

> "Beloved, do not believe every spirit, but test the spirits to see whether they are from God, because many false prophets have gone out into the world. By this you know the Spirit of God: every spirit that confesses that Jesus Christ has come in the flesh is from God; and every spirit that does not confess Jesus is not from God; this is the spirit of the antichrist, of which you have

heard that it is coming, and now it is already in the world." (1 John 4:1–3; cp. 2 John 7)

Against docetism, orthodox, biblical Christianity equally affirms *both* the Lord's deity *and* his humanity. And necessarily so. As we see in John's statement above, he deems Jesus' material humanity as essential for the Christian faith: "every spirit that confesses that Jesus Christ has come in the flesh is from God; and every spirit that does not confess Jesus is not from God" (1 John 4:2). In fact, we believe that Jesus was 100% God and 100% man, and not a mixture of the two natures, diluting one for the other.

Jesus has a Human Body

We all are very much aware of his historical birth because Christmas exercises such a big impact every year in our calendar. The New Testament record is clear: his mother Mary gives birth to him like any other mother bears a son (Luke 2:7; cp. Matt 1:21; Gal 4:4). He becomes flesh in order to dwell in this world: "the Word became flesh, and dwelt among us, and we saw His glory, glory as of the only begotten from the Father, full of grace and truth" (John 1:14). He even grows and develops like any normal child (Luke 2:40, 52).

Jesus himself affirms his own humanity by calling himself a man: "you are seeking to kill Me, a man who has told you the truth" (John 8:40). In fact, his preferred self-reverential title is "the Son of Man," which occurs eighty-two times in the New Testament (Matt 8:20; 9:6; 10:23; 11:19; 12:8, 32; 13:37, 41; 16:13; etc.). This title shows his connection to mankind.

Not only so, but Jesus is recognized as a man by all who see him (Matt 8:27; 12:24; 13:56; 26:61; 27:47; John 6:52; 7:12; 19:5; Acts 2:22). Only at his transfiguration does his deity become visible and alter his appearance (Matt 17:2; Mark 9:2; Luke 9:29). And as a man he is a physical being who can be touched (Luke 24:39; John 20:27; 1 John 1:1).

While he is on earth, his human body is subject to all the weaknesses of our physical bodies. We read in the Gospels that Jesus wearies (John 4:6), hungers (Matt 4:2), eats (Luke 24:42), sleeps (Matt 8:24), suffers (Heb 5:8), bleeds (Luke 22:44; John 19:34), and dies (John 18:32; 19:30; 1 Cor 15:3) just as we do. God cannot undergo such in his divine nature; Jesus' full humanity accounts for these.

Salvation Requires a Human Savior

Though it is essential that Jesus be divine in order to save sinners, he also has to be human. For several reasons it is necessary for him to be human, firmly connected with the human race. In his *Systematic Theology*,[1] Wayne Grudem provides several reasons why the fully human nature of Christ is necessary. I will summarize his arguments.

Because he joins himself to the human race and becomes one of us, by his ministry he is able to accomplish:

Representative obedience. Jesus is fully human so that he can stand in our place as our representative in order to live out a perfect life in our behalf. Just as Adam represents us in his original testing, so Christ represents us in his life-long testing which results in his full obedience. Paul drives this point home in a clear and compelling fashion, drawing parallels between Adam who fails and Jesus who succeeds:

> "So then as through one transgression there resulted condemnation to all men, even so through one act of righteousness there resulted justification of life to all men. For as through the one man's disobedience the many were made sinners, even so through the obedience of the One the many will be made righteous." (Rom 5:18–19)

Substitutionary sacrifice. In his eternal nature as God, Jesus could not suffer and die for us. He specifically takes upon himself a true human body and soul in order to endure God's just punishment for sin.

As God Jesus could not die; as an angel he would not be able to stand in our place, representing us before God. Therefore, the writer of Hebrews explains that:

> "since the children share in flesh and blood, He Himself likewise also partook of the same, that through death He might render powerless him who had the power of death, that is, the devil, and might free those who through fear of death were subject to slavery all their lives. For assuredly He does not give help to angels, but He gives help to the descendant of Abraham." (Heb 2:14–16)

---

[1] Wayne Grudem, *Systematic Theology: An Introduction to Biblical Doctrine* (Grand Rapids: Zondervan, 1994).

This is because "He had to be made like His brethren in all things, so that He might become a merciful and faithful high priest in things pertaining to God, to make propitiation for the sins of the people. For since He Himself was tempted in that which He has suffered, He is able to come to the aid of those who are tempted." (Heb 2:17–18)

The necessity of his taking up a human body is a crucial point which Hebrews repeatedly makes. For instance, later we read:

"For it is impossible for the blood of bulls and goats to take away sins. Therefore, when He comes into the world, He says, 'sacrifice and offering you have not desired, but a body you have prepared for me; in whole burnt offerings and sacrifices for sin you have taken no pleasure. then I said, "Behold, I have come (in the scroll of the book it is written of me) to do your will, O God."'After saying above, 'sacrifices and offerings and whole burnt offerings and sacrifices for sin you have not desired, nor have you taken pleasure in them' (which are offered according to the law), then he said, 'Behold, I have come to do your will.' He takes away the first in order to establish the second. By this will we have been sanctified through the offering of the body of Jesus Christ once for all." (Heb 10:4–10)

Mediatorial labor. A mediator is a person who intervenes between two parties "in order to initiate a relationship . . . or effect a reconciliation."[2] Because of our sin "we were enemies" to God (Rom 5:10), "alienated and hostile" to him (Col 1:21) and thereby "having no hope" (Eph 2:12). But Jesus comes as our mediator to bring us back to a right relationship with the Father: "there is one God, and one mediator also between God and men, the man Christ Jesus, who gave Himself as a ransom for all, the testimony given at the proper time" (1 Tim 2:5–6).

And again, Hebrews speaks to this point: "He is the mediator of a new covenant, so that, since a death has taken place for the redemption of the transgressions that were committed under the first covenant, those who have been called may receive the promise of the eternal inheritance" (Heb 9:15).

Calling fulfillment. God creates man in his image and places him in the Garden of Eden to begin his high calling as God's image in exercising

---

[2] "Mediation, mediator" in Paul J. Achtemeier, *HarperCollins Bible Dictionary* (San Fransico: HarperSanFransico, 1996), 666.

dominion over all of creation (Gen 1:26–27). Because of his sin, though, God banishes Adam from the Garden and curses him, causing him to labor by the sweat of his brow against a resistant creation (Gen 3:17–19).

In order to bring man back to his righteous calling, Jesus comes to fulfill this purpose. Regarding man's failed role and Jesus' fulfillment we read:

> "'You have put all things in subjection under his feet.' For in subjecting all things to him, He left nothing that is not subject to him. But now we do not yet see all things subjected to him. But we do see Him who was made for a little while lower than the angels, namely, Jesus, because of the suffering of death crowned with glory and honor." (Heb 2:8–9)

Thus, Paul teaches that God "put all things in subjection under His [Jesus'] feet, and gave Him as head over all things to the church" (Eph 1:22).

Righteous example. Since we are fallen we have no perfect examples among us showing how we should live. But as the perfect Man, Jesus lives a life of example for us. Jesus teaches his disciples: "For I gave you an example that you also should do as I did to you" (John 13:15). Though this refers to his specific example of serving others as he washes his disciples' feet (John 13:12–24), we must understand the larger point of this example: following him in humbly serving God in all of life.

John presents this as the Christian's moral and spiritual obligation: "the one who says he abides in Him ought himself to walk in the same manner as He walked" (1 John 2:6). We are to strive to apply his Word by his Spirit while "being transformed into the same image" (2 Cor 3:18). In fact, God predestines us to be "conformed to the image of His Son" (Rom 8:29).

Sympathetic love. We cannot complain that God does not know what it is like to be a frail human dwelling in the dust of the earth. And because he was fully human and living in the same world we do, Jesus is able to sympathize with us in all our temptations: "since He Himself was tempted in that which He has suffered, He is able to come to the aid of those who are tempted" (Heb 2:18).

Indeed, "we do not have a high priest who cannot sympathize with our weaknesses, but One who has been tempted in all things as we are, yet without sin. Therefore let us draw near with confidence to the throne of grace, so that we may receive mercy and find grace to help in time of need" (Heb 4:16).

Paradigmatic resurrection. Jesus not only redeems us from our sin but enters into the resurrection state before us. We can look to his resurrection experience as the paradigm for our own. We know that the Lord's actual body was resurrected from the tomb as a reanimated material body (Luke 24:39; John 20:27). Paul speaks of the Lord's entering into his resurrection body functioning as "the first fruits" of our own future resurrection (1 Cor 15:23). That is, like the first crop of harvest shows the fact and nature of the harvest to come, so Jesus' resurrection anticipate ours. Jesus undergoes death and is resurrected from the dead to serve as "the first-born from the dead" (Col 1:18).

As a consequence, we know that our redemption is full, involving both body and soul. Our resurrected bodies will be physically raised imperishable, possessing great glory and power (1 Cor 15:43-44). Paul also teaches that we will be raised as a "spiritual body" (1 Cor 15:44). This does not mean our resurrection bodies will be composed of immaterial spirit. Our "spiritual body" is no more made of spirit than a Coke bottle is made of Coke. Rather, it means that our bodies will now be animated with the fulness of the Spirit, no longer subject to and hampered by animal appetites, as in our "soulish [natural] bodies".[3]

Thus, the full humanity of Christ is necessary for our salvation: "God displayed [him] publicly as a propitiation in His blood through faith. This was to demonstrate His righteousness, because in the forbearance of God He passed over the sins previously committed; for the demonstration, I say, of His righteousness at the present time, so that He would be just and the justifier of the one who has faith in Jesus" (Rom 3:25–26).

Because Jesus is both God and man — the theanthropos[4] —, we may have confidence that:

---

[3] Paul sets our current "natural [lit. soulish, Gk. *psuchikon*] bodies over against our future "spiritual [*pneumatikon*] bodies," thereby contrasting their *controlling principles* rather than their *compositional makeup*. See: Kenneth L. Gentry, Jr., "Christ's Resurrection and Ours," *Chalcedon Report* (April, 2003): 10ff.

[4] This technical term is rooted in a compound of two Greek words: *theos* is the word for "God" (from which we get our word "theology"); *anthropos* is the word for "man" (from which we derive "anthropology").

Jesus is a Perfect Savior

As noted previously man is a sinner who has broken God's Law: "everyone who practices sin also practices lawlessness; and sin is lawlessness" (1 John 3:4). In fact, "whoever keeps the whole law and yet stumbles in one point, he has become guilty of all" (Jms 2:10). And as a consequence of his law-breaking, man is alienated from God (Col 1:21). This is because God is holy and righteous (Isa 45:19) and cannot look favorably upon sin (Hab 1:13).

So then, we need a perfect Savior who can fully keep God's Law, which is "holy and righteous and good" (Rom 7:12). And since Jesus is God the Son who becomes truly man, he enters the human race and can live out God's Law under our circumstances and in our behalf. This allows our righteous and just God to have Jesus represent us before him so that he might apply his righteousness to our accounts.

God's word teaches us that Jesus perfectly keeps God's Law. Therefore, he could challenge his opponents to point out any sin (law-breaking) in his life. In fact, he publically asks them: "Which one of you convicts Me of sin?" (John 8:46).

Indeed, he was confident of his perfect sinlessness and could therefore resolutely declare: "I have kept My Father's commandments and abide in His love" (John 15:10). He quite strongly emphasizes his sinlessness: "He who sent Me is with Me; He has not left Me alone, for I *always do* the things that are pleasing to Him" (John 8:29). The present tense verb "I do" speaks of continual action. He accentuates this by adding the adverb of time *pantote*, which means "always, at all times, on every occasion."

Paul speaks of Christ's sinlessness and his redemptive work in our behalf by noting that God "made Him who knew no sin to be sin on our behalf, so that we might become the righteousness of God in Him" (2 Cor 5:21). Peter agrees with Paul when he speaks of Jesus "who committed no sin, nor was any deceit found in his mouth" and who consequently "bore our sins in His body on the cross, so that we might die to sin and live to righteousness" (1 Pet 2:22, 24; cp. Isa 53:12; Heb 9:28).

In Hebrews we learn that Jesus "has been tempted in all things as we are" he was "yet without sin" (Heb 4:15). This letter also emphatically states that Jesus is our ultimate high priest who is "innocent, undefiled, separated from sinners and exalted about the heavens" (Heb 7:26).

Given all that is required for salvation — a human-divine Savior who fully keeps God's Law in behalf of his people — we should not be surprised to learn that:

Jesus is the Only Savior

As we continue our study of *The Truth about Salvation* we must recognize an important element for which our holy faith is severely criticized: its *exclusivism*. By this we mean that biblical Christianity holds that God saves only those who are in covenant with him through Jesus Christ. Thus, Christianity is exclusivistic: entry into heaven is not open to all men on a variety of bases.

Orthodox Christianity's exclusivism clashes head-on with the modern politically-correct approach to all matters moral, social, and religious. Unfortunately though, liberal (unorthodox) branches of Christianity exist, which strive to be politically-correct in arguing for universal openness.[5] Ligonier Ministries well expresses the problem we face: "In our postmodern, relativistic age, Christians who believe what Jesus said about being the sole Mediator of redemption . . . are often seen as narrow-minded, bigoted, and mean-spirited. Even professing evangelicals are increasingly apt to deny this foundational Christian claim."[6]

Christian liberalism (including more subtle liberalizing tendencies even within evangelicalism) is simply humanism in Christian dress. Or as Jesus might put it: it is a wolf in sheep's clothing. Regarding the offer of salvation we must recognize two basic approaches within liberal theological circles.

(1) *Inclusivism*. Some liberals argue for religious inclusivism, which holds that God will save all men because he is their Creator. Creaturely status before God is what God accepts.

(2) *Pluralism*. Others promote religious pluralism, which argues that God will save all who humbly seek him through any religion. Sincere yearning for God is what God accepts.

---

[5] I would concur with the famed early twentieth-century theologian J. Gresham Machen who argued that liberal Christian theology is not Christian at all. His book is still in print in a new edition: J. Gresham Machen, *Christianity and Liberalism* (Grand Rapids: Eerdmans, 2009).

[6] "One Way of Salvation," Ligonier Ministries. http://www.ligonier.org/learn/devotionals/one-way-of-salvation/

True Christianity, however, is a revealed religion rather than a philosophical construct. Thus, it is governed by God's Word rather than by man's thoughts. It has set truth claims rather than evolving notions of truth and right. And in Christianity's revealed record we discover that it is clearly, specifically, and necessarily exclusivistic. Ron Nash has published an excellent analysis of these three views while defending exclusivism: *Is Jesus the Only Savior?*[7]

We learn that Christianity is exclusivistic from Christ himself. Jesus dogmatically asserts: "I am the way, and the truth, and the life; no one comes to the Father but through Me" (John 14:6). Thus, he warns that "he who does not honor the Son does not honor the Father who sent him" (John 5:23). And "he who rejects Me rejects the One who sent Me" (Luke 10:16). And "he who rejects Me and does not receive My sayings, has one who judges him; the word I spoke is what will judge him at the last day" (John 12:48). If we reject Christ's teaching why would we call ourselves "Christians"? Such does not make sense.

Because of this, in their earliest gospel preaching the Apostles could declare the same truth. Preaching in Jerusalem (Acts 4:5), Peter proclaims: "there is salvation in no one else; for there is no other name under heaven that has been given among men by which we must be saved" (Acts 4:12). He very obviously rejects pluralism, for he is warning the Jews that following their religious notions (in Judaism) is ineffective: they need to believe in Christ.

To the church at Corinth Paul writes: "For no man can lay a foundation other than the one which is laid, which is Jesus Christ" (1 Cor 3:11). He clearly rejects inclusivism for he does not believe all men will be saved, for he writes: "This is good and acceptable in the sight of God our Savior, who desires all men to be saved and to come to the knowledge of the truth. For there is one God, and one mediator also between God and men, the man Christ Jesus" (1 Tim 2:3–5).

Conclusion

Christianity offers true salvation by means of a perfect Savior, Jesus Christ the Lord. He is a perfect Savior because he is God in the flesh — the God-man — who comes to give his life as a ransom for us.

---

[7] Ron Nash, *Is Jesus the Only Savior?* (Grand Rapids: Zondervan, 1994).

Christianity differs from the other two major, monotheistic world religions: Judaism and Islam. It differs on the fundamental question of salvation. Christianity is a redemptive religion (wherein God saves sinners through his Son), whereas Judaism and Islam are moralistic religions (wherein God receives sinners on the basis of their own efforts).

But how do men receive the salvation God provides in Jesus? This leads us to our next chapter.

REVIEW QUESTIONS FOR DISCUSSION

These questions deal directly with the material in this chapter. The answers can be found in the chapter.

1. Why is it important that the Savior be man in addition to his being God?
2. What was "docetism" in the ancient church? What are some biblical evidences against this doctrinal error?
3. What are some evidences from Scripture that Jesus was truly man?
4. What do we mean by Jesus' "representative obedience"? What are some verses that affirm this doctrine?
5. What do we mean by the "substitutionary sacrifice" of Jesus? What are some verses that affirm this doctrine?
6. What do we mean by the "mediatorial labor" of Jesus? What are some verses that affirm this doctrine?
7. How is Jesus' resurrection important to understanding our own resurrection?
8. How is the Law of God significant in understanding the significance of Jesus' humanity and our salvation?
9. What are some theological views of the result of salvation as it applies to the human race?
10. What are some evidences from Scripture that prove that those who are saved must exercise a direct affirmation of Jesus as Savior?

STRETCHING FURTHER

These questions are designed to promote further group reflection on the topic beyond that which is presented in the chapter above.

1. What are some technical theological terms that speak of the union of the deity and humanity of Christ in one person?
2. In addition to docetism, what are some other errors involving the denial of the true humanity of Christ?
3. How could Christ endure the eternal wrath of God in the short time in which he was on the cross?
4. Can you name any theologians who are Inclusivists? Pluralists? Exclusivists?
5. Have you read any articles or books on the debate between the three views represented in the last question?

Chapter 7
SALVATION IS BY FAITH ALONE

As we continue our study of *The Truth about Salvation* we must recall our previous lessons. We have seen, though a loving God creates us (ch. 1), we have become grievous sinners (ch. 2) who deserve our righteous God's judgment and wrath (ch. 3). But God is such a gracious God (ch. 4) that in the person of Jesus Christ he takes human nature upon himself and offers himself as a sacrifice for sins in our behalf (chs. 5–6).

But now the question becomes: *How* do we receive his salvation? After all, we understand that Christianity is exclusivistic (ch. 6), holding that not all men will be saved. Does not Jesus himself teach that men must "fear Him [God] who is able to destroy both soul and body in hell" (Matt 10:28)? And that men must "enter through the narrow gate; for the gate is wide and the way is broad that leads to destruction, and there are many who enter through it. For the gate is small and the way is narrow that leads to life, and there are few who find it" (Matt 7:13–14)? Therefore, the liberal doctrines of pluralism and inclusivism contradict the biblical revelation regarding salvation.

Upon hearing of the necessity of salvation, the Jews listening to Peter and the 120 disciples on Pentecost are driven to ask in desperation: "Brethren, what shall we do?" (Acts 2:37). We all must ask the Philippian jailer's question to Paul and Silas: "Sirs, what must I do to be saved?" (Acts 16:31).

These questions are very important for those who desire to be saved, and to know that we are saved. And it is vitally important for us if we desire to show others the way of salvation (a major concern of this book). So then: how *do* fallen sinners lay hold of salvation in Christ? The Reformation, which Martin Luther sparks in the 1500s, answers this question: Salvation comes to the sinner by grace through faith alone.

The Requirement of Faith

Since God sends his Son to effect salvation, and since we are sinners who cannot save ourselves, the Bible urges us simply — but truly and deeply — to accept salvation by faith alone. This is the constant message of the New Testament apostles and evangelists who build on Christ's own teaching.

During the Reformation the Reformers reject the teachings of the Roman Catholic Church on many issues, and particularly regarding salvation. In rejecting Rome they promote what we today summarize in Latin as the "five solas." That is, we may rightly characterize the salvation taught in the New Testament revelation as: "Sola Scriptura" ("by Scripture alone"), "Sola Gratia" ("by grace alone), "Sola Fide" ("by faith alone"), "Solus Christus" ("by Christ alone"); and is "Soli Deo Gloria" ("glory to God alone").

Our focus in this section will be on Sole Fide. This is the message we must present to sinners regarding what they must do to be saved.

Faith Proclaimed in the Old Testament

Though Judaism had corrupted God's message of salvation long before the time of Christ, God himself had always saved sinners by faith. We see this most clearly in Moses' record of Abraham. Moses says of him that "he believed in the LORD; and He reckoned it to him as righteousness" (Gen 15:6).

In fact, the New Testament points us back to Abraham as the great exemplar of saving faith, as the father of believers, Abraham's example is picked up frequently in the New Testament. Perhaps the earliest book in the New Testament is James. We find James (the brother of Jesus, Gal 1:19; Jude 1) stating that "Abraham believed God, and it was reckoned to him as righteousness" (Jms 2:23).

Paul the great Apostle to the Gentiles (Rom 11:13; 1 Tim 2:7) refers to Abraham's example quite often. In one of his earliest epistles, Galatians, Paul specifically declares: points out that "Abraham believed God, and it was reckoned to him as righteousness" (Gal 3:6).

In his heavily theological masterpiece, Romans, Paul elaborates on this historical truth. He asks what he deems to be an obvious question, then offers a clear and direct answer: "what does the Scripture say? 'Abraham believed God, and it was credited to him as righteousness'" (Rom 4:6; citing Gen 15:6). Just a few verses later he adds: "for this reason it is by faith, in order that it may be in accordance with grace, so that the promise will be guaranteed to all the descendants, not only to those who are of the Law, but also to those who are of the faith of Abraham, who is the father of us all" (Rom 4:16).

Peter declares that salvation by faith is the message of the Old Testament prophets: "Of Him all the prophets bear witness that through His name everyone who believes in Him receives forgiveness of sins" (Acts 10:43).

Early in Romans Paul proves salvation by faith from the Old Testament in opening his letter to the Romans: "for in it the righteousness of God is revealed from faith to faith; as it is written, 'but the righteous man shall live by faith'" (Rom 1:16–17, citing Hab 2:4). In fact, New Testament writers frequently cited Habakkuk 2:3 and 4 in promoting faith (Rom 1:16–17; Gal 3:11; Heb 10:37–38). Several chapters later Paul cites Isaiah 28:16: "just as it is written, 'Behold, I lay in Zion a stone of stumbling and a rock of offense, and he who believes in him will not be disappointed." Peter also cites this verse (1 Pet 2:6).

As he closes Romans, Paul refers once again to the Old Testament as evidence of faith for salvation: "Now to Him who is able to establish you according to my gospel and the preaching of Jesus Christ, according to the revelation of the mystery which has been kept secret for long ages past, but now is manifested, and by the Scriptures of the prophets, according to the commandment of the eternal God, has been made known to all the nations, leading to obedience of faith" (Rom 16:25–26).

The writer of Hebrew provides an entire lengthy chapter listing examples of faith in the Old Testament. In that chapter "by faith" appears eleven times as he provides one example after another. In fact, early on in his epistle he laments those who are lost in the Old Testament because they lacked faith: "we have had good news preached to us, just as they also; but the word they heard did not profit them, because it was not united by faith in those who heard" (Heb 4:2).

Faith Proclaimed in Jesus' Ministry

The clarifying and promoting of salvation by faith begins anew in Christ's own preaching. It is a recurring theme in his ministry, and is especially emphasized in John's Gospel. Consider the following texts:

> John 1:12: "As many as received Him, to them He gave the right to become children of God, even to those who believe in His name."

> John 3:15–16, 18: "Whoever believes will in Him have eternal life. For God so loved the world, that He gave His only begotten Son, that whoever believes in Him shall not perish, but have

eternal life. . . . He who believes in Him is not judged; he who does not believe has been judged already, because he has not believed in the name of the only begotten Son of God. "

John 3:36: "He who believes in the Son has eternal life; but he who does not obey the Son will not see life, but the wrath of God abides on him."

John 5:24: "Truly, truly, I say to you, he who hears My word, and believes Him who sent Me, has eternal life, and does not come into judgment, but has passed out of death into life."

John 6:35: "I am the bread of life; he who comes to Me will not hunger, and he who believes in Me will never thirst."

John 8:24: "Therefore I said to you that you will die in your sins; for unless you believe that I am He, you will die in your sins."

On and on we could go. But we must skip close to the end of John's Gospel to see his goal in writing it. John 20:30–31 reads: "many other signs Jesus also performed in the presence of the disciples, which are not written in this book; but these have been written so that you may believe that Jesus is the Christ, the Son of God; and that believing you may have life in His name."

Faith Proclaimed by the Apostles

Peter preaches salvation through faith at the Jerusalem Council: "we believe that we are saved through the grace of the Lord Jesus, in the same way as they also are" (Acts 15:11). Paul is the great "Apostle of Faith," who repeatedly emphasizes salvation by faith. Perhaps the clearest and most dramatic example is when the Philippian jailer approaches him about how to be saved: "he said, 'Sirs, what must I do to be saved?' They said, 'Believe in the Lord Jesus, and you will be saved, you and your household'" (Acts 16:30–31).

In his Epistle to the Romans Paul repeatedly speaks of salvation by faith, even linking it to the strongest word for forgiveness of sin: "propitiation."[1] He speaks of Christ Jesus "whom God displayed publicly as a propitiation in His blood through faith. This was to demonstrate His

---

[1] Propitiation speaks of the turning away of God's wrath by God's paying the price through pouring his wrath on his son, Jesus Christ.

righteousness, because in the forbearance of God He passed over the sins previously committed; for the demonstration, I say, of His righteousness at the present time, so that He would be just and the justifier of the one who has faith in Jesus" (Rom 3:25–26).

In Romans 5:1 he writes: "therefore having been justified by faith, we have peace with God through our Lord Jesus Christ." Romans 10:9 reads: "if you confess with your mouth Jesus as Lord, and believe in your heart that God raised Him from the dead, you will be saved."

Many others verses declare faith as the means of salvation: Acts 8:12; 10:43; Romans 3:22; 4:5, 24; 16:26; 1 Corinthians 15:17; Galatians 2:16, 20; 3:2–9, 22, 26; Ephesians 2:8; 3:17; Philippians 3:9; Colossians 2:11–12; 2 Thessalonians 2:13; 1 Timothy 1;16; 2 Timothy 1:12; 3:15; Hebrews 10:22, 38–39; 11:6; 1 Peter 1:5–9; 2:6; 1 John 5:1, 5,13.

The Rejection of Works

Faith is so central to salvation that the New Testament rejects all notion of meritorious works, which are almost universally proclaimed in moralistic religions. Paul vehemently rejects all notion of works righteousness: "I do not nullify the grace of God; for if righteousness comes through the Law, then Christ died needlessly" (Gal 2:21). In fact, he writes: "For we maintain that a man is justified by faith apart from works of the Law" (Rom 3:28).

A Mistaken View

Unfortunately, some theologians, including evangelical and Reformed representatives, argue that Paul's denunciation of the works of the Law is not a rejection of attempted works righteousness. Rather it actually rejects the Jewish concern for keeping ritual laws that serve as "nationalistic boundary markers" or identity badges for inclusion in the covenant community of Israel. Those boundary-markers include such rituals as circumcision, Sabbath-keeping, clean food laws, and so forth. Romans 3:28 is a key verse in this line of thinking: "we maintain that a man is justified by faith apart from works of the Law."

Paul's rejection of the works of the Law, however, involves more than this. It involves all efforts at keeping the Law for the purpose of earning salvation, whether keeping ceremonial boundary markers or specific moral laws. We will focus briefly on Romans 3:28 to demonstrate the error in this boundary-marker approach.

First, Romans 3:28 appears in connected context. Romans 1–3 is teaching that all men are sinners and the sin is a universal problem, not simply a Jewish concern. He is dealing with the predicament of Jew and Gentiles (Rom 1:16; 29–10; 3:9, 29). Second, the doers of the Law include Gentiles who would have no concern for Jewish boundary markers (Rom 2:13–14). In fact, their doing of the Law is deemed "instinctive" (Rom 3:13) which certainly does not speak of ceremonial laws.

Third, Paul rebukes the Jews for not keeping the moral law: "you, therefore, who teach another, do you not teach yourself? You who preach that one shall not steal, do you steal? You who say that one should not commit adultery, do you commit adultery?" (Rom 2:21–22). Fourth, he specifically declares that both Jews and Greeks re under sin" for "there is none righteous, not even one" (Rom 3:9, 10). He even states that "whatever the Law says, it speaks to those who are under the Law, so that every mouth may be closed and all the world may become accountable to God" (Rom 3:19).

The Proper view

Clearly Paul is not rebuking ethnic pride when he discounts the "works of the Law." Rather, he is concerned with blatant legalism, the idea that a man can keep enough of the Law to merit favor with God. We can see this in numerous references that have nothing to do with ceremonial concepts.

Perhaps the most famous passage discounting works-righteousness is Ephesians 2:8–9: "For by grace you have been saved through faith; and that not of yourselves, it is the gift of God; not as a result of works, so that no one may boast." But we find several others such passages in Paul's writings.

> "If Abraham was justified by works, he has something to boast about, but not before God" (Rom 4:2).

> "To the one who does not work, but believes in Him who justifies the ungodly, his faith is reckoned as righteousness" (Rom 4:5).

> "But if it is by grace, it is no longer on the basis of works, otherwise grace is no longer grace" (Rom 11:6).

He "has saved us and called us with a holy calling, not according to our works, but according to His own purpose and grace which was granted us in Christ Jesus from all eternity" (2 Tim 1:9).

"He saved us, not on the basis of deeds which we have done in righteousness, but according to His mercy, by the washing of regeneration and renewing by the Holy Spirit, whom He poured out upon us richly through Jesus Christ our Savior, so that being justified by His grace we would be made heirs according to the hope of eternal life" (Tit 3:5–7).

The Capacity to Believe

We must deal with one last issue in this matter of God's gracious salvation by faith in Christ. As noted previously (ch. 2), the Bible teaches that man is such a depraved sinner that he cannot even come to Christ for salvation: "No one can come to Me unless the Father who sent Me draws him; and I will raise him up on the last day" (John 6:44; cp. John 6:65). Or as he puts it elsewhere: "Truly, truly, I say to you, unless one is born again he cannot see the kingdom of God" (John 3:3). How then can they even exercise faith?

God's grace is such that he even grants faith to depraved sinners. The New Testament teaches this most clearly in Ephesians 2:8–9:

> "For by grace you have been saved through faith; and that not of yourselves, it is the gift of God; not as a result of works, so that no one may boast. For we are His workmanship, created in Christ Jesus for good works, which God prepared beforehand so that we would walk in them."

Ligonier Ministries explains this text quite well:

> "Faith is something that we exercise, and so some Christians think we bring this to the table when we are saved. They think we work faith up in ourselves and that all people are born with the ability to do so. Ephesians 2:8 makes this view impossible. The grammatical gender of the demonstrative this in "this is not your own doing" must refer back to the entire complex of things Paul mentions in the verse — salvation, grace, and faith. It is true that we are the ones who put our faith in Christ, but God gives us this faith and guarantees that we will exercise it unto salva-

tion. If the Holy Spirit changes our hearts, we will not refuse the call to trust in Christ."[2]

Similarly we read in Philippians 1:29: "to you it has been granted for Christ's sake, not only to believe in Him. . . ." God grants the sinner the capacity to believe. The sinner is "dead in trespasses and sins" (Eph 2:1), and cannot believe on his own. Thus, we read of Lydia's conversion to Christ that "the Lord opened her heart to respond to the things spoken by Paul" (Acts 16:14).

Likewise, in 2 Timothy 2:25 we hear Paul's prayer that "God may grant them repentance leading to the knowledge of the truth." God grants repentance; men do not work it out themselves. Repentance and faith are inextricably linked in true conversions. Paul explains his ministry by noting that he testifies "of repentance toward God and faith in our Lord Jesus Christ" (Acts 20:21). Repentance is "from dead works," whereas "faith [is] toward God" (Heb 6:1).

All of this theology of conversion roots back in Christ's own teaching: "This is the work of God, that you believe in Him whom He has sent" (John 6:29). For this reason, Jesus is "the author and perfecter of faith" (Heb 12:2).

This should be encouraging to us as we present the gospel. God opens the heart of the spiritually-dead sinner; men do not do so through knowledge, wisdom, or persuasive power. As Paul states: "our gospel did not come to you in word only, but also in power and in the Holy Spirit and with full conviction" (1 Thess 1:5). Though the sinner is spiritually dead and therefore incapable of exercising faith, God gives new life so that he may: sinners are born again by God's grace in that they "were born, not of blood nor of the will of the flesh nor of the will of man, but of God" (John 1:13).

---

[2] Ligonier Ministries, http://www.ligonier.org/learn/devotionals/grace-alone-through-faith-alone/

The Truth about Salvation

REVIEW QUESTIONS FOR DISCUSSION

These questions deal directly with the material in this chapter. The answers can be found in the chapter.

1. What are the five "solos" promoted today by evangelical Protestants? What does each one mean?
2. What evidence do we have that, despite the first-century Pharisees, God had always required faith for salvation — even in the Old Testament? Cite some verses.
3. Who is the Old Testament's greatest example of faith? Why do you say that?
4. What are some of the clearest examples from Jesus' teaching of the centrality of the call to faith in salvation?
5. Which of the four Gospels shows the heaviest focus on faith in salvation? What is the stated goal of that Gospel?
6. What are some key verses that you would use to show someone they must believe in Christ to be saved?
7. Some scholars argue that Paul's rejection of "the works of the Law" speaks of his rejection of the peculiarly Jewish elements of the Law that set Jews off from Gentiles. What are some reasons showing that this is a mistaken view?
8. What is "legalism"? What verses undermine legalism?
9. How are faith and repentance related? How are they different?
10. How can a "dead in trespasses" unbeliever end up believing in Christ? Cite verses supporting your answers.

STRETCHING FURTHER

These questions are designed to promote further group reflection on the topic beyond that which is presented in the chapter above.

1. What chapter in the New Testament is popularly recognized as "The Hall of Faith"?
2. What does John 1:13 by each of the elements listed: "not of blood nor of the will of the flesh nor of the will of man"?

3. In your view does faith precede regeneration (thereby leading to it)? Or is faith the immediate result of regeneration (which causes faith)? Support your answer.
4. What does Paul mean when he says to the Philippian jailer: "believe in the Lord Jesus, and you will be saved, you *and your household*" (Acts 16:30–31)?
5. If God "gives/grants" salvation, how is it the sinner's obligation to believe?

Chapter 8
SALVATION IS A LIFE CHANGER

As we continue our study of *The Truth about Salvation*, we must understand the living principle characterizing salvation. God's saving us from our sins does not simply list our names in the Heavenly Register, the Lamb's Book of Life (Phil 4:3; Heb 12:23; Rev 3:5; 21:27). Nor does it only secure our future destiny in heaven (2 Cor 5:1; Col 1:5; 1 Pet 1:4). Of course, when saved we are recorded in the Lamb's Book of Life and are destined to heaven. But salvation has a continuing, active impact on our lives in the present.

Two Evangelical Viewpoints

In evangelical circles we discover two approaches to the impact of salvation on the Christian's life. Though the debate between the two positions had long simmered in the Twentieth Century, it really exploded in the evangelical worlds in the 1990s with the release of John MacArthur's book *The Gospel according to Jesus* (1988).

The most widely-held view is known as the "free grace" or "faith only" view. It is called "easy believism" by its opponents, who see it as reducing the gospel. The other view is known as "Lordship salvation." This was the view MacArthur presented in his book. Of course, many theologians engaged the debate, but MacArthur is the one who really re-opened the question.

Free Grace Salvation

The Free Grace view holds that the initial act of believing in Christ does not involve committing one's life to him. Rather saving faith in Christ simply receives him as Savior alone without simultaneously receiving him as Lord. This view unlinks justification and sanctification, arguing that the convert to Christ does not *necessarily* grow in grace by means of sanctification. Its advocates understand the significance of the debate as follows:

Charles Ryrie brings the point of contention to the fore in his *Balancing the Christian Life*:

> "The importance of this question cannot be overestimated in relation to both salvation and sanctification. The message of faith only and the message of faith plus commitment of life cannot both be the gospel; therefore, one of them is false and comes under the curse of perverting the gospel or preaching another gospel (Gal. 1:6-9)."[1]

Robert Lightner agrees: "These views — the absolutely free gift view and the lordship view — cannot both be right. They are mutually exclusive."[2]

Zane Hodges comments on the debate, focusing on the idea of "faith":

> "Over a period of many years the idea has gained ground that true saving faith is somehow distinguishable from false kinds of faith, primarily by means of its results or 'fruits.' Thus two men might believe exactly the same things in terms of content, yet if one of them exhibited what seemed to be a 'fruitless' Christian experience, his faith would be condemned as 'intellectual assent,' or 'head belief' over against 'heart belief.' In a word, his faith was false faith — it was faith that did not, and could not, save. . . . In every other sphere of life, except religion, we do not puzzle ourselves with introspective questions about the 'nature' of our faith."[3]

One of the leading theologians in the Free Grace movement is the late Dr. Zane Hodges. He wrote several books explaining, promoting, and defending the doctrine. He even titles one of his books: *Absolutely Free!*.[4]

Lordship Salvation

The Lordship view holds to the necessity of acknowledging Christ as the Lord and Master of one's life in the act of truly believing in Him as Savior. These are not two different, sequential acts (or successive steps), but rather one act of pure, trusting faith.

---

[1] Charles C. Ryrie, *Balancing the Christian Life* (Chicago: Moody, 1969), 170.

[2] Robert P. Lightner, *The Savior, Sin, and Salvation* (Nashville: Thomas Nelson, 1991), 200.

[3] Zane C. Hodges, *Absolutely Free! A Biblical Reply to Lordship Salvation* (Grand Rapids: Zondervan, 1989), 27.

[4] Hodges, *Absolutely Free!*.

As MacArthur notes, the basic issue has to do with "what Scripture means when it speaks of faith."[5] Lordship advocacy fully endorses salvation by grace through faith, but in a different way than do Free Grace Salvation advocates. It believes that true faith involves commitment rather than the mere acceptance of the truth of Christ and his benefits. As John Gerstner argues: "The question is not whether good works are necessary to salvation, but in what way are they necessary. As the inevitable outworking of saving faith, they are necessary for salvation. As the meritorious ground of justification, they are not necessary *or acceptable*."[6] No works are pre-requisite for salvation (2 Tim 1:9; Eph 2:8–9), but neither is true salvation devoid of work (Jms 2).

Generally speaking, the Free Grace Salvation advocates present Christ as Savior to be accepted by faith only, devoid of any idea of commitment to Him. The average Non-Lordship churchman can often by heard witnessing with such words as: "Give Jesus a chance." "Suppose His claims are false, what have you lost?" "Try God." "Let go and let God." Faith in Christ tends to be little more than accepting the facts of His deity and atonement apart from any idea of obeying Him.

True Faith

To properly understand *The Truth about Salvation* it is important to have an adequate grasp of what saving faith truly is. In order to do this, we must look at the original Greek terminology used in the New Testament. The three most common Greek words that speak of faith are the verb *pisteuō* (which occurs 242 times in the New Testament) and the nouns *pistis* (which occurs 243 times) and *pistos* (which occurs sixty-seven times).

Frederick Danker's Greek lexicon gives the concept involved in the noun *pistis* as "trust, confidence, faith."[7] It defines the verb *pisteuō* thus: "to entrust oneself to an entity in complete confidence, *believe (in), trust,*

---

[5] John D. MacArthur, "Faith According to the Apostle James," *Journal of the Evangelical Theological Society*, 33 (March, 1990): 13.

[6] John H. Gerstner, *Wrongly Dividing the Word of Truth: A Critique of Dispensationalism* (Brentwood, Tenn.: Wolgemuth & Hyatt, 1991), 210.

[7] Frederick William Danker, *A Greek-English Lexicon of the New Testament and Other Early Christian Literature* (3d. ed.: Chicago: University Press, 2000), 818.

[with] implication of total commitment to the one who is trusted."[8] W. E. Vine further adds regarding *pisteuō*: It is "to believe, also to be persuaded of, and hence, to place confidence in, to trust, signifies, in this sense of the word, reliance upon, not mere credence."[9]

With these definitions before us, we must ask: what kind of trust or reliance is it that does not obey? To trust Jesus Christ, the Lord of the universe, must involve submission to him as personal Lord and Master. One cannot be relying on Christ if he chooses to chart his own life course in opposition to the Lord from the very outset of his faith relationship.

As the *Theological Dictionary of the New Testament* well notes: "in as much as trust may be a duty, *pistos* can come to have the nuance of 'obedient.'"[10] It correlates the relationship of New Testament faith with that of the Old Testament, showing that both revolve around obedience. This, it notes, is particularly emphasized in the great chapter of faith, Hebrews 11.[11] In each of the examples in "the Hall of Faith" in Hebrews 11 we find examples of the *obedient action* of faith.

Faith is clearly related to obedience (Greek: *hupakoē*) in Paul's theology. Faith to Paul is "obedience to the gospel" (*hupokouein to euaggeliō*, Rom 10:16; cp. 2 Thess 1:7–8). Paul praises the Roman church at the outset of his epistle because its "faith is spoken of throughout the world" (Rom 1:8). At the close of Romans he associates faith with obedience by repeating his first statement in a parallel thought: "your obedience is come abroad to all men" (Rom 16:19). He even says in 1 Corinthians 1:17 that his ministry is "to preach the gospel," whereas in Romans 15:18 he says it is "to make the gentiles obedient." In short, Paul speaks freely of obedient faith as being the way of salvation (Rom 1:5; 6:17; 16:26; cp. Acts 6:7; Heb 11:8). Thus, faith binds a man in trusting obedience to Christ the Lord.

In Hebrews 5:9 we read that Jesus "became the author of eternal salvation unto all them that obey him." As Stott well states: "the bended

---

[8] Danker, *Lexicon*, 817.

[9] W. E. Vine, *An Expository Dictionary of New Testament Words* (Old Tappan, N. J.: Revell, 1941), 1:116.

[10] *Pisteuō*" in Gerhard Kittel, ed., *Theological Dictionary of the New Testament*, trans. by Geoffery W. Bromiley (Grand Rapids: Eerdmans, 1968), 6:175.

[11] *Theological Dictionary of the New Testament*, 6:205.

knee is as much a part of saving faith as the open hand."[12] Christ is the Christian's Master; when one believes in Christ he is bound to Him in an obedient, vital relationship. Commitment is an essential element in the act of believing. Faith is not merely intellectual assent.

In both Jesus' teaching and His experience with respondents, we have evidence of false, uncommitted faith in some, and true, submissive faith in others. And the respondents initially seem to be responding to the same exact message in identical ways. But we learn that there is a qualitative difference, despite those opposed to Lordship Salvation doctrine.

For instance, in the Kingdom Parables we have several illustrations of falsely-professing, non-converted people involved in the kingdom of heaven. These are distinguished from true members of the kingdom. We think of the tares among the wheat (Matt 13:24–30) and the bad fish among the good (Matt 13:47–50). The Lord even tells us that these are responding to the same preached word — and some even appear initially to demonstrate the same salvation. In the Parable of the Sower the *same word* is received, but in different ways (Matt 13:4–9). Only the fruitful reception is the true reception; the other apparent receptions turn out to be false (Matt 13:18–33). Jesus presents the false converts as tares and bad fish; the true as wheat and good fish.

In John 2:23 we learn that many "believe" in Christ. But Jesus refuses to commit himself to them — a rather remarkable response to new believers: "when He was in Jerusalem at the Passover, during the feast, many believed in His name, observing His signs which He was doing. But Jesus, on His part, was not entrusting Himself to them, for He knew all men" (John 2:23–24). By all external appearance these are true believers. But Jesus knows their hearts! Their believing is not a true believing.

In the case of Judas, who undoubtedly was lost (John 6:70–71; Acts 1:25), we learn of the confidence of the other disciples in his "belief." For a time it appears to be genuine: "Then Jesus said to *the twelve* [including Judas], 'Do you also want to go away?' Then Simon Peter answered Him, 'Lord, to whom shall we go? You have the words of eternal life. Also *we* [including Judas] have come to believe and know that You are the Christ, the Son of the living God" (John 6:67–69). Despite Peter's confidence in the belief of "the twelve," Jesus knows the heart: "Jesus answered them,

---

[12] John R. W. Stott, "Must Christ Be Lord to Be Savior — Yes!," *Eternity* 10:9 (September, 1959): 13ff.

'Did I not choose you, the twelve, and one of you is a devil?' He spoke of Judas Iscariot, the son of Simon, for it was he who would betray Him, being one of the twelve" (John 6:70-71).

In John 8:30 we read: "As He spoke these words, many believed in Him." But as in John 2:23–24 and John 6:67–71, Christ's analysis of their alleged faith exposes its true nature:

> "Then Jesus said *to those Jews who believed Him*, 'If you abide in My word, you are My disciples indeed. And you shall know the truth, and the truth shall make you free.' They answered Him, 'We are Abraham's descendants, and have never been in bondage to anyone. How can you say, "You will be made free"?' Jesus answered them, 'Most assuredly, I say to you, whoever commits sin is a slave of sin. And a slave does not abide in the house forever, but a son abides forever. Therefore if the Son makes you free, you shall be free indeed. I know that you are Abraham's descendants, but you seek to kill Me, because My word has no place in you. . . . You do the deeds of your father.' Then they said to Him, 'We were not born of fornication; we have one Father, God.'" (John 8:31–37, 41)

Elsewhere we see additional examples of false, empty, uncommitted faith. Simon Magus is said to believe (Acts 8:13a), and on that basis he is baptized (Acts 8:13b). But a short time later (Acts 8:14), Peter declares that he is to "perish" because he is not truly among the redeemed and needs to repent: "But Peter said to him, 'Your money perish with you, because you thought that the gift of God could be purchased with money! You have neither part nor portion in this matter, for your heart is not right in the sight of God. Repent therefore of this your wickedness, and pray God if perhaps the thought of your heart may be forgiven you. For I see that you are poisoned by bitterness and bound by iniquity." (Acts 8:20–23)

John notes in his First Epistle that even antichrists had been accepted among the believers: "Little children, it is the last hour; and as you have heard that the Antichrist is coming, even now many antichrists have come, by which we know that it is the last hour. They went out from us, but they were not of us; for if they had been of us, they would have continued with us; but they went out that they might be made manifest, that none of them were of us" (1 John 2:18–19). Notice he clearly states that had these antichrists truly been "of us" they would have "continued with us." They did not persevere in their professed faith in Christ. Hence, the danger of "false brethren" (2 Cor 11:26; Gal 2:4).

The Nature of Salvation

James powerfully teaches that faith will evidence itself in vitality and works (Jms 2:14–26). We are justified by faith, but that faith is never alone — it will evidence itself by its living, active nature. James is speaking of "evidential justification," justification showing itself by good works. Evidential justification is sanctification in action. It is vitally related to Lordship salvation, for when one truly, savingly believes in Christ as Savior *and* Lord, his life will evidence the fact of regeneration, the receiving of new life.

Far too many people claim to believe in Christ as Savior, while at the same time living as if he never existed. This acceptance does as much for one's own soul as did Tetzel's selling of papal indulgences in the Sixteenth Century. All faith is not saving faith; empty faith is too often promoted today.

Because of the principle of self-preservation (Eccl 3:11), men may shrink from the prospect of eternal hell and accept an escape route of easy belief. But not being under true conviction of the Holy Spirit, they do not want to be saved from sin and self to live holy unto God. Faith is a life principle (Heb 11; Jms 2; Rom 1:17), which in its binding nature directs one's confidence and trust into the *person* of Christ the Lord.

The reason we may expect fruit and continuance over the long run by the truly redeemed is because of the very change God works in us. The true believer is not acting unaided, when he believes. Neither is he receiving an *addition to* his life. True salvation involves a radical *change within* his life and from above. Note the following.[13]

1. The Bible says the Christian is blessed with "every spiritual blessing" (Eph 1:3). God's "divine power has granted to us everything pertaining to life and godliness, through the true knowledge of Him who called us by His own glory and excellence" (2 Pet 1:3).

2. We are under the power of grace, not of sin: "sin shall not be master over you, for you are not under law but under grace" (Rom 6:14).

---

[13] For more information, see: Kenneth L. Gentry, Jr., *Lord of the Saved: Getting to the Heart of the Lordship Debate* (Chesnee, SC: Victorious Hope, 2016).

3. The Holy Spirit and Christ indwell us: "you are not in the flesh but in the Spirit, if indeed the Spirit of God dwells in you. But if anyone does not have the Spirit of Christ, he does not belong to Him" (Rom 8:9; cp. 1 Cor 3:16; 6:19; 2 Cor 6:16; Gal 2:20).

4. Through the sovereign action of God, the Christian is spiritually resurrected and made alive: "When you were dead in your transgressions and the uncircumcision of your flesh, He made you alive together with Him, having forgiven us all our transgressions" (Col 2:13; cp. John 5:2, 24; Rom 6:4–9). Thus, the Christian has a new life: "Truly, truly, I say to you, he who hears My word, and believes Him who sent Me, has eternal life, and does not come into judgment, but has passed out of death into life" (John 5:24; cp. John 3:36; 6:67; 1 John 5:11).

5. We have at all times Christ above us interceding for us: "who is the one who condemns? Christ Jesus is He who died, yes, rather who was raised, who is at the right hand of God, who also intercedes for us." (Rom 8:34; cp. Heb 7:25) This passage ties together his death and his intercession for us. Is his death effective? Why not His intercession? In fact, "we know that no one who is born of God sins; but He who was born of God keeps him, and the evil one does not touch him" (1 John 5:18). The sinning here is the present active indicative in Greek. It indicates habitual action. Because of Christ's work for and in us, we cannot live in habitual rebellion against God.

6. The Christian has a new heart or character (Eze 36:26; cp. Eze 11:19) from the moment of regeneration. He, therefore, is a "new man" (Eph 4:22–24; Col 3:9–10) and a "new creation" (2 Cor 5:17; Gal 6:15; Eph 2:10).

Conclusion

True faith brings a change of life. It is not an inert acceptance of facts, but a deep, heartfelt commitment of life. The person who savingly believes in Christ as Savior also accepts him as Lord. This is why Paul sternly warns professing believers: "test yourselves to see if you are in the faith; examine yourselves! Or do you not recognize this about yourselves, that Jesus Christ is in you — unless indeed you fail the test?" (2 Cor 13:5).

For this reason also, John teaches that "no one who is born of God practices sin, because His seed abides in him; and he cannot sin, because he is born of God" (1 John 3:9). By this he does not mean a truly born-again believer never sins. After all, he opens his epistle by stating that "if we say that we have no sin, we are deceiving ourselves and the truth is not in us" (1 John 1:8). Rather in 1 John 3:9 he means that the born again believer does not live *habitually* in sin as he did *before* he professed Christ.

James says: "faith without works is useless" (Jms 2:20). Faith is living, productive, and fruitful. This does not amount to perfectionism (living a perfectly sinless life), eradicationism (the eradication of the sin nature), synergism (redemption by the aid of man), or autosoterism (self-salvation).

There are important reasons we may expect fruitfulness and continuance over the long run for the truly redeemed. These are related to the very supernatural operations of salvation. The true believer is not acting unaided, when he believes. Neither is he receiving an addition to his life. True salvation involves a change in his life

REVIEW QUESTIONS FOR DISCUSSION

These questions deal directly with the material in this chapter. The answers can be found in the chapter.

1. What are the two basic evangelical approaches to salvation by grace? Briefly summarize each position.
2. Are justification and sanctification linked? If they are, how are they linked? If not, why not?
3. Are good works in any way essential to salvation? Explain your answer.
4. Does faith entail obedience in any way? Explain and document your answer.
5. How are the Kingdom Parables in Matthew 13 helpful to the debate over salvation?
6. Explain how Judas' situation in the Gospel record helps us better understand the nature of faith.
7. List some New Testament examples of empty faith that is less than saving faith.
8. James 2:14 seems to speak of salvation on the basis of good works. How should this text be understood?

9. How can preaching the doctrine of hell sometimes be counterproductive to calling men to faith?
10. Explain how true salvation expects a change of life. Use Scripture.

STRETCHING FURTHER

These questions are designed to promote further group reflection on the topic beyond that which is presented in the chapter above.

1. Name three leading, published proponents of each of the two basic evangelical approaches to salvation. Have you read any of their works?
2. The Greek word for believe and faith are *pistis* and *pisteuō*. They are related to the word *peithō*. What does this word mean. How is significant to the evangelical debate of Lordship salvation?
3. What is a Greek lexicon, and how is it helpful for studying the New Testament?
4. What does perfectionism teach?
5. What is autosoterism?

Chapter 9
SALVATION IS ETERNALLY SECURE

In that salvation comes to us be means of God's sovereign grace, we should expect that it will be maintained by the exercise of that same divine grace. And, as a matter of fact, the Scriptures do teach the eternal security of the saints. Though this doctrine has been abused in the easy-believism community, it is a glorious comfort for the true believer.

Eternal Security Defined

In the Westminster Confession of Faith we find an excellent statement on the meaning and nature of eternal security. The Confession subsumes eternal security under the broader doctrine of the perseverance of the saints (which also covers the doctrine we present in ch. 8 above).

> WCF 17:1. "They, whom God has accepted in His Beloved, effectually called, and sanctified by His Spirit, can neither totally nor finally fall away from the state of grace, but shall certainly persevere therein to the end, and be eternally saved."
>
> WCF 17:2. "This perseverance of the saints depends not upon their own free will, but upon the immutability of the decree of election, flowing from the free and unchangeable love of God the Father; upon the efficacy of the merit and intercession of Jesus Christ, the abiding of the Spirit, and of the seed of God within them, and the nature of the covenant of grace: from all which arises also the certainty and infallibility thereof."
>
> This doctrine is well-summarized by Peterson who writes:
>
> "Salvation is the work of God alone. On the cross, Jesus secured the salvation for those who would believe in Him. This makes salvation an act of God, because God is the one who initiates, consummates, and sustains salvation by His power for His glory. Persevering to the point of glorification is the natural end to the given salvation, which is incomplete and meaningless without

perseverance. God cannot fail and those that He saves will be given a new body at the resurrection of the saints in the last days, to spend eternity in Heaven. This is the great doctrine of eternal security."[1]

But before we present the biblical argument for eternal security, we must warn of the potential danger of misapplying the doctrine. So let us consider:

Eternal Security Danger

Before we present the biblical arguments for eternal security, we must recognize that this hope is for only those who are truly born again. As we note in chapter 8, salvation necessarily produces a life-changing effect on the born-again sinner. After all, salvation brings "new life" (Rom 6:4; cp. Rom 7:6; 8:11; Col 3:10) and is rooted in a "new covenant" which writes God's Law on the heart (Jer 31:31–34; cp. Rom 8:1–9; 2 Cor 3:3). Consequently, we must understand eternal-security doctrine in the expectation that the truly regenerate will tend to live for Christ, will tend to grow in grace — even though they often stumble.

The easy-believism approach (which is embodied in the "Free Grace" movement) to eternal security is dangerous in several respects, however. I will quickly state four areas of danger.

First, eternal security advocacy (wrongly understood) can become a crass lure to attract sinners. Free Grace advocacy often presents the prospect of eternal security as a tempting lure to the unconverted. The hope of eternal life is appealing to man, who has eternity in his heart (Eccl 3:11) and who recognizes death to be his enemy (1 Cor 15:26). And the sinner who cannot understand the things of God (1 Cor 2:14) can be drawn to an offer of a salvation that comes with no obligations.

Second, eternal security advocacy (wrongly understood) can offer confidence to those who are not truly saved.[2] Few writers have put the danger more pointedly than Arthur Pink: "A promise misapplied will be

---

[1] Greg Peterson, "Eternal Abuse: The Biblical Promise of Eternal Security and its Abuse within Free Grace Theology" (May 1, 2013), 1. https://www.academia.edu/4977566/ETERNAL_ABUSE_The_Biblical_Promise_of_Eternal_Security_and_its_Abuse_within_Free_Grace_Theology

[2] For a helpful study of the dangers in this regard, see: Peterson, "Eternal Abuse."

a seal upon the sepulcher, making them sure in the grave of sin, wherein they lay dead and rotting." Many within evangelical circles show no interest in the things of God (such as the Bible, worship, prayer, fellowship, or service). Yet they take comfort in believing: "Well, at least I am saved." Their lives show no evidence of the Spirit within, and they can only point back to a point in time where they "prayed the sinner's prayer." Yet, they were taught in the context of their evangelistic encounter that all they had to do was to believe, then heaven was certainly their destiny — no matter what.

We see this danger lurking in such statements as the following by Free Grace advocates:

R. B. Thieme writes:

"It is possible, even *probable*, that when a believer out of fellowship falls for certain types of philosophy, if he is a logical thinker, he will become an 'unbelieving believer.' Yet believers who become agnostics are still saved; they are still born again. You can even become an *atheist*; but if you once accepted Christ as Savior, you cannot lose your salvation, even though you deny God."[3]

A similar statement is found in Ryrie's writing: "Normally one who has believed can be described as a believer; that is, one who continues to believe. But . . . a believer may come to a place of not believing, and yet God will not disown him, since He cannot disown Himself."[4]

Third, eternal security advocacy (wrongly understood) can undermine the integrity of the church. As MacArthur complains: "the cheap grace and easy faith of a distorted gospel are ruining the purity of the church. The softening of the New Testament message has brought with it a putrefying inclusivism that in effect sees almost any kind of positive response to Jesus as tantamount to saving faith."[5] When they church pulls in too many who are not truly converted, the very life of the church is diminished. The church can become a tare field rather than a wheat field.

Fourth, eternal security advocacy (wrongly understood) can destroy the witness of Christianity. Christians are called to glorify our Father who

---

[3] R. B. Thieme, *Apes and Peacocks, of the Pursuit of Happiness* (Houston, Tex.: Berachah Church, 1973), 23.

[4] Charles C. Ryrie, *So Great Salvation* (Wheaton, Ill.: Victor, 1989), 141.

[5] John F. MacArthur, Jr., *The Gospel according to Jesus* (Grand Rapids: Zondervan, 1988), p. 37.

is in heaven (Matt 5:16). In order to accomplish that task, Christ calls us to be the "salt of the earth," but if the Christian community is bloated with non-regenerate men "it is no longer good for anything, except to be thrown out and trampled under foot by men" (Matt 5:13).

This is a serious problem in Christian circles today. That the problem is real is demonstrated in the fact that L. S. Chafer could refer to "the great mass of carnal Christians" and Ryrie worries about Lordship advocacy by questioning: "Where is there room for carnal Christians?"[6] Ray Stedman bemoans "how much the spirit of carnality has invaded the church."[7]

Many that they might call ""carnal" are perhaps false professors, having only an inadequate knowledge of the truth at best. Hodges admits "To be sure, there is much reason to think that there are multitudes of people in churches today who have never really been saved."[8]

Eternal Security Data

Certainly eternal security doctrine carries with it the potential for abuse. What doctrine does not?[9] Nevertheless, it is clearly taught in Scripture and is a great source of comfort to God's true people. We can see this glorious doctrine in numerous passages and from various angles.

Salvation wording

Perhaps one of the most easily overlooked evidences for eternal security is really the most obvious. It appears in the very wording used to speak of salvation. The common phrase "eternal life" appears forty-one times in the New Testament and carries within it the very necessity of

---

[6] Lewis Sperry Chafer, *Grace: The Glorious Theme* (Grand Rapids: Zondervan, 1922, 1950), 346. Ryrie, *Balancing the Christian Life*, 170.

[7] Ray Steadman, "Carnal and Spiritual Christians," Authentic Christianity website. http://www.raystedman.org/new-testament/1-corinthians/carnal-and-spiritual-christians

[8] Hodges, *Absolutely Free!*, p. 19.

[9] Paul shows that God's saving grace can lead some to surmise that they may "continue in sin so that grace may increase" (Rom 6:1). Indeed, even the glorious Scriptures can be distorted and bring destruction upon the unstable (2 Pet 3:16).

eternal security. After all, "eternal life" must continue eternally, and not just for a time.

The Bible's best known verse serves as strong evidence for eternal security. In John 3:16 we hear our Lord declare that "God so loved the world, that He gave His only begotten Son, that whoever believes in Him shall not perish, but have eternal life." This verse demands eternal security on several bases:

(1) In the Greek, the verb "have" (Gr. *echē*) appears in the present tense. This requires an ongoing, continuous reality for those who "have" eternal life. (2) Jesus expressly calls the result "eternal" life. If the life lasted but for a time until lost, it would not be "eternal." (3) Jesus specifically states that the (true) believer "shall *not* perish." All three factors in this statement demand that the condition of the true believer is eternally secure.

We see this same truth in other verses declaring the presence of "eternal life." Consider, for instance, the following three statements.

> "He who believes in the Son has eternal life; but he who does not obey the Son will not see life, but the wrath of God abides on him" (John 3:36).

> "Truly, truly, I say to you, he who hears My word, and believes Him who sent Me, has eternal life, and does not come into judgment, but has passed out of death into life" (John 5:24).

> "For the wages of sin is death, but the free gift of God is eternal life in Christ Jesus our Lord" (Rom 6:23).

Promise result

Jesus promises that it is God's will for him to bring sinners to the resurrection: "this is the will of Him who sent Me, that of all that He has given Me I lose nothing, but raise it up on the last day" (John 6:39). Note four ways by which this confirms eternal security:

1. He declares that what he is about to say "is the will of Him who sent Me," i.e., God. Thus, whatever he is about to promise is rooted in God's will — it does not depend upon man.

2. He informs us that God actually gives *people* to him for a certain purpose. He does not state that God simply tenders an offer of something for people to consider, but that he actually gives the people themselves for that purpose.

3. Of "all" the people whom the Father gives to him, Christ promises that he will "lose nothing." Not one will be lost in the transaction. And finally:

4. He promises that he will "raise it up on the last day."

Thus, the very will of God involves his giving specific people to Christ, and Christ promises that he will not lose one of them but will bring them safely to the resurrection on the last day.

Double protection

Not only may we discover verses promising eternal life and security for the believer, but we even hear some that apply that security equally to both God the Father and God the Son. Consider John 10:27–29:

> "Jesus answered them, 'I told you, and you do not believe; the works that I do in My Father's name, these testify of Me. But you do not believe because you are not of My sheep. My sheep hear My voice, and I know them, and they follow Me; and I give eternal life to them, and they will never perish; and no one will snatch them out of My hand. My Father, who has given them to Me, is greater than all; and no one is able to snatch them out of the Father's hand.'"

This remarkable passage is packed with evidence for the believer's security:

1. Christ calls those who hear and follow him "My sheep" of whom he says: "I give eternal life to them." So once again we hear the Lord using the language of eternity regarding the life that he grants in salvation. And once again:

2. He states that "they will never perish." This should be expected by the very nature of the life being "eternal." So this statement emphatically declares his point by doubly confirming it: they will "never perish" because they have "eternal life." And if that is not enough, then consider that he powerfully proclaims:

3. "No one will snatch them out of My hand." Jesus' statement is not abstract, but concrete. His people are not names in a ledger, but persons protected in his hand. And no one is able to overpower Christ and pry his hand open to pull them away from his protective custody. But once again we find an emphatically doubling of the imagery, for he adds:

4. "No one is able to snatch them out of the Father's hand." That hand of Christ is sufficient to hold us. But in his imagery we are not only in Christ's hand, but in the Father's hand. How much more secure can one be than in the hand of Christ and in the hand of God?

Spiritual insurance

Paul brings another spiritual image to bear on the matter of security: that of sealing. In Ephesians 1:13–14 we learn of our spiritual insurance: "In Him, you also, after listening to the message of truth, the gospel of your salvation — having also believed, you were sealed in Him with the Holy Spirit of promise, who is given as a pledge of our inheritance, with a view to the redemption of God's own possession, to the praise of His glory."

Note the powerful security involved here.

1. The believer is "sealed in Him." The idea of sealing involves the secure protecting of the contents of that which is sealed (e.g., see Rev 5:1–5). Thus, later in the same epistle Paul states that we are not to grieve the Holy Spirit of God because by him "you were sealed for the day of redemption" (Eph 4:30). He reiterates this once again in his last epistle: "the firm foundation of God stands, having this seal, 'The Lord knows those who are His'" (2 Tim 2:19).

2. We are not only sealed "in Him" but "with the Holy Spirit of promise." This sealing is not by some earthly judge or king, but by Jesus and the Holy Spirit of God. Indeed, he is the Holy Spirit "of promise."

3. The Holy Spirit not only seals us but is himself "a pledge of our inheritance, with a view to the redemption of God's own possession." Though we are sinners who cannot live perfectly in this world, the Holy Spirit indwelling us gives us a foretaste of our future life in the presence of God: he is a "pledge" of that future "inheritance" involving "redemption." What we have now in part, is a token of what we will have in full in eternity.

Eternal plan

In the writings of Paul we find repeated emphasis on the ultimate starting point of our salvation. Our redemption is rooted in the eternal plan of God, not in the temporal activity of man.

We read a forceful statement on this in Ephesians 1:4–5: "He chose us in Him before the foundation of the world, that we would be holy and blameless before Him. In love He predestined us to adoption as sons through Jesus Christ to Himself, according to the kind intention of His will." Since our salvation was planned from all eternity past, it predestines us to God for all eternity future. We truly have "eternal" security coming and going.

Because of this truth Paul can present us with a "golden chain" linking eternity past to eternity future in our salvation:

"We know that God causes all things to work together for good to those who love God, to those who are called according to His purpose. For those whom He foreknew, He also predestined to become conformed to the image of His Son, so that He would be the firstborn among many brethren; and these whom He predestined, He also called; and these whom He called, He also justified; and these whom He justified, He also glorified" (Rom 8:28–30).

Here we see that God has "His purpose" operating in our salvation. And it operates in behalf of those "whom He foreknew," that is, whom he fore-loved. The biblical conception of "knowing" often speaks of a deeply personal knowledge of intimacy, i.e. it speaks of love (Gen 4:1, 17, 25; Hos 13:5; Amos 3:2; Matt 7:22–23; Gal 4:9; 2 Tim 2:19[10]). Those whom he foreknew/foreloved he "predestined," and those whom he predestined he called, then justified, and then glorified (in his plan the future is always before him). God's predestination leads to our inevitable glorification. And this truly requires *eternal* security.

Conclusion

The Bible is abundantly clear: God loves his people with an everlasting love. An everlasting love that lasts . . . forever. His love begins in eternity past in his plan and continues into eternity future in his presence.

At the historical point in time when we come to salvation we receive :*eternal* life. Eternal life is by definition eternally secure, or else it would

---

[10] In some of the Old Testament passages, the Hebrew word "know" appears, but is translated as "love" or "chose" or some other affectionate term. For instance, in Amos 3:2 the NASB translated "known" as "chosen."

The Truth about Salvation

not be deemed "eternal." Born again Christians can depend upon God's plan, Jesus' promise, and God and Jesus' activity to secure us forever.

REVIEW QUESTIONS FOR DISCUSSION

These questions deal directly with the material in this chapter. The answers can be found in the chapter.

1. How would you define the biblical doctrine of eternal security?
2. How is the doctrine of eternal security abused in the "Free Grace" approach to salvation?
3. Discuss how the phrase "eternal life" is helpful to proving the eternal security of the believer.
4. Discuss John 6:39 and its usefulness to proving the eternal security of the believer.
5. Discuss John 10:27–29 and its usefulness to proving the eternal security of the believer.
6. Discuss how the "sealing" of the Spirit helps prove the eternal security of the believer.
7. Discuss how God's sovereignty in election helps prove the eternal security of the believer.
8. List a few helpful verses for proving eternal security other than those mentioned in questions 4 and 5.
9. Do you believe that good and true doctrines can be abused by pushing them too far? Give an example.
10. What do you believe to be the strongest biblical argument for eternal security?

STRETCHING FURTHER

These questions are designed to promote further group reflection on the topic beyond that which is presented in the chapter above.

1. What is the Westminster Confession of Faith? Explain where it came from and what its purpose is.
2. What is a "carnal Christian" in the Free Grace/Easy-believism scheme?

3. What is "Arminianism" and "Calvinism," and how does each approach understand the question of eternal security?
4. What are some verses used against the doctrine of eternal security? How would you answer someone using these against eternal security?
5. Have you always believed in eternal security since becoming a Christian? Or has your view changed over time? What changed you (if you did alter you position).

Chapter 10
CHRISTIANS HAVE A GLORIOUS DESTINY

As we continue studying *The Truth about Salvation* we come now to see the *consequences* of salvation. Salvation does not simply involve some internal feeling or psychological satisfaction that comes with receiving Christ. It has enormous, long-range implications for the life of the saved.

As we consider our glorious destiny as God's redeemed "vessels of mercy" (Rom 9:23), we must look at our future on earth, in heaven, and in eternity. So let us begin by noting the significance of:

Our Current Calling

Unfortunately, some Christians are "so heavenly minded that they are no earthly good." Too many do not think about the implications of salvation for daily living. Too few recognize the core reality of their new life in Christ and its expected impact on their daily affairs.

To really grasp our calling in the world, we must understand the significance of creation. To do this we must reflect on creation not only as the *activity* of God in creating, but the *result* of his creating: God creates the material world (Gen 1; Neh 9:6). For this reason Scripture frequently calls God "Creator" (e.g., Eccl 12:1; Isa 27:11; 40:28; Rom 1:25; 1 Pet 4:19). In his creative work he provides us with physical bodies (Gen 2:7; Isa 45:12) and places us in the world so that we might enjoy it (Eccl 5:18–19; 1 Tim 6:17).

To equip us for life in this material world, God provides us with wonderfully-designed bodies to adeptly engage in physical labor (Psa 139:14). We recognize, of course, that labor becomes difficult because of the Fall of Adam (Gen 3:17–19). Nevertheless, labor itself is a calling from God that begins in pre-Fall Eden (Gen 2:15). In fact, it is one of the three creation ordinances that serve as perpetual obligations on man in the world. Those three ordinances are:

> Marriage, designed for man's happiness and to propagate the human race (Gen 1:26–27; 2:23–24; Matt 19:4–6).

Labor, designed to engage man's productive mental and physical capabilities (Gen 1:26–27; 2:15; Prov 10:4).

Sabbath, designed to allow rest from his labor as well as the opportunity for corporately worshiping God (Gen 2:1–3; Exo 20:9–11).

Regarding labor, wise Solomon informs us that "there is nothing better for a man than to eat and drink and tell himself that his labor is good. This also I have seen that it is from the hand of God" (Eccl 2:24). He also states: "I know that there is nothing better for them than to rejoice and to do good in one's lifetime; moreover, that every man who eats and drinks sees good in all his labor — it is the gift of God (Eccl 3:12–13[1]). Sadly, modern American culture is becoming more oriented to play rather than work.

Because of this creation ordinance, Christians should enjoy life on earth and develop its potentialities in the service and to the glory of God. In fact, God creates us in his image for this very purpose: as God creates and governs all things, we must reflect him by exercising dominion in his world (Gen 1:25–27; 5:1; Psa 8:4–9).

Christ even prays for his disciples' labor and service in the world as he prepares to leave them:

> "I do not ask You to take them out of the world, but to keep them from the evil one. They are not of the world, even as I am not of the world. Sanctify them in the truth; Your word is truth. As You sent Me into the world, I also have sent them into the world. For their sakes I sanctify Myself, that they themselves also may be sanctified in truth." (John 17:15–19)

Indeed, since "the earth is the Lord's, and all it contains" (Psa 24:1), we must strive to honor God in all of our activities on earth. Paul commands us that "whether, then, you eat or drink or whatever you do, do all to the glory of God" (1 Cor 10:31). Elsewhere he writes: "Whatever you do, do your work heartily, as for the Lord rather than for men, know-

---

[1] The key to understanding Ecclesiastes is to recognize that Solomon is comparing life-perspectives or worldviews. He shows the vanity of life when viewed from "below the sun" without reference to God (Eccl 1:4, 13–14). Whereas, the glory and happiness of life comes to those who view things from God's perspective above the sun: "The conclusion, when all has been heard, is: fear God and keep His commandments, because this applies to every person" (Eccl 12:13; cp. Eccl 2:24; 3:13; 5:19).

ing that from the Lord you will receive the reward of the inheritance. It is the Lord Christ whom you serve" (Col 3:23–24). And because of our eternal destinies, we know that our "toil is not in vain in the Lord" (1 Cor 15:58).

Of course, not only are we to creatively and productively labor in the world, but we are to labor in the gospel. Jesus teaches that the gospel creates the kingdom of God on earth, for he links the gospel with the kingdom: "Now after John had been taken into custody, Jesus came into Galilee, preaching the gospel of God, and saying, 'The time is fulfilled, and the kingdom of God is at hand; repent and believe in the gospel'" (Mark 1:14–15). And since the Scripture teaches that "the gospel is the power of God for salvation" (Rom 1:16), we can have hope in its victory in the world.

Jesus expressly teaches this in his large teaching material that we know as the Kingdom Parables. The parables of the mustard seed and of the leaven both indicate the kingdom's growth and influence in the world:

> "He presented another parable to them, saying, 'The kingdom of heaven is like a mustard seed, which a man took and sowed in his field; and this is smaller than all other seeds, but when it is full grown, it is larger than the garden plants and becomes a tree, so that the birds of the air come and nest in its branches.' He spoke another parable to them, 'The kingdom of heaven is like leaven, which a woman took and hid in three pecks of flour until it was all leavened.'" (Matt 13:31–32)

Both of these parables promise us the large scale growth and worldwide dominance of the gospel. Not only so, but they also call us to recognize the gradual, long-term development of the kingdom principle. God's will is for the kingdom to grow gradually like a seed (cp. Mark 4:26–29), and to penetrate slowly like leaven. But in both images we see a final glorious result: a "tree" that dominates the whole garden and "leaven" that penetrates all the meal.

Christians, we are *not* on the losing side in history. After all, did not Jesus teach us to pray confidently: "'Your kingdom come. /Your will be done, / On earth as it is in heaven" (Matt 6:10)? Did he not also give us what we call the Great Commission, which is his formal commission to disciple *all nations*?

"Jesus came up and spoke to them, saying, 'All authority has been given to Me in heaven and on earth. Go therefore and make disciples of all the nations, baptizing them in the name of the Father and the Son and the Holy Spirit, teaching them to observe all that I commanded you; and lo, I am with you always, even to the end of the age.'" (Matt 28:18–20)

Thus, you should live out your salvation with a view to the future, historical progress of Christianity in the world. In order to do this, Christians must "work out your salvation with fear and trembling; for it is God who is at work in you, both to will and to work for His good pleasure" (Phil 2:12). That is, you must work salvation into all of your life, not just hold it in the privacy of your heart. And you must trust that God works through you to do his will.

Those who know *The Truth about Salvation* must therefore challenge the world with a full-orbed Christian worldview. For ourselves, we must listen to Paul's urging: "by the mercies of God, to present your bodies a living and holy sacrifice, acceptable to God, which is your spiritual service of worship. And do not be conformed to this world, but be transformed by the renewing of your mind, so that you may prove what the will of God is, that which is good and acceptable and perfect" (Rom 12:1–2).

To apply the implications of our salvation to the world, we must take up Paul's call to "destroy speculations and every lofty thing raised up against the knowledge of God" by "taking every thought captive to the obedience of Christ" (2 Cor 10:5). After all, God gave his Word to equip us so that we "may be adequate, equipped for *every* good work" (2 Tim 3:17). Our salvation brings with it a new perspective on life, an outlook submissive to Christ and his Word.

For these reasons, the Lord calls us to be "the light of the world," and "a city set on a hill" (Matt 5:14). Christians, *The Truth about Salvation* presents a glorious hope for future history.

But now let us note that beyond this temporal realm, God gives us the sure hope of:

Our Heavenly Life

Contrary to the materialistic, evolutionary science of the day, man is not simply a chance collection of molecules, little more than matter in motion. In 1967 Harvard University Professor of Biology George Wald (1906–1997) won The Nobel Prize in Physiology for Medicine 1967. He expressed this viewpoint well when he was once asked who in his view Shakespeare was. He answered: "a chance collection of molecules that existed 400 years ago."[2]

Christianity believes man is more than a material creature, more than "a chance collection of molecules." We hold that we have a dual nature, being composed of both matter and spirit united in one being. We see this from the very moment of our creation: "The LORD God formed man of dust from the ground, and breathed into his nostrils the breath of life; and man became a living being [Heb.: "soul"]" (Gen 2:7).

Consequently, when we die "the dust [material body] will return to the earth as it was, and the spirit will return to God who gave it" (Eccl 12:7). For this reason, Jesus warns of the double danger of unbelief: "Do not fear those who kill the body but are unable to kill the soul; but rather fear Him who is able to destroy both soul and body in hell" (Matt 10:28). As the Christian maxim puts it: "Born twice, die once; born once, die twice."[3]

Because we have a spiritual component to our being, when we die we suffer a separation of body from soul (or spirit) as the immaterial soul enters into heaven. Unlike the materialist, we do not believe we cease to exist and simply vanish away at death. Rather, the Christian enters a new sphere of existence. In fact, even the unsaved enter into a new sphere, but in their case it is eternal hell (Matt 25:46; Mark 9:47–48; Rev 14:10–11).[4] But *The Truth about Salvation* teaches that the spirit of the believer is saved by the grace of God and enters into heaven at death.

But now, what is heaven? And how do we know we have that glorious destiny before us after this life?

In its most fundamental sense, heaven is the place of the special presence of God. It is true, though, that God is omnipresent, which means

---

[2] Francis A. Schaeffer, *How Should We Then Live? The Rise and Decline of Western Thought and Culture* (Old Tappan, N.J.: Revell, 1967), 164.

[3] We do not have to wonder with the comedian: "Why don't born again people have two belly buttons?"

[4] In this book about salvation we will not focus on the doctrine of hell. For a helpful study on the reality of hell, we recommend the following works: Robert A. Peterson, *Hell on Trial: The Case for Eternal Punishment* (Nutely, N.J.: P&R, 1995) and Christopher W. Morgan and Robert A. Peterson, *Hell Under Fire: Modern Scholarship Reinvents Eternal Punishment* (Grand Rapids: Zondervan, 2007).

that he exists everywhere, fully and simultaneously (1 Kgs 8:27; Psa 139:7–16; Jer 23:24). But the Bible teaches that in an important sense God's special focal presence is in heaven. For this reason, God himself declares to Isaiah: "Heaven is My throne" (Isa 66:1; cp. Psa 11:4; 103:19; Matt 5:34; 23:22). And Jesus teaches us to pray: "Our Father who is *in heaven*" (Matt 6:9; cp. Matt 7:11, 21; 10:32–33).

In fact, Jesus himself is currently no longer in this world because he entered heaven long ago. Acts 1 records his ascension into heaven: "after He had said these things, He was lifted up while they were looking on, and a cloud received Him out of their sight" (Acts 1:9). Regarding this, the angels said to the disciples: "This Jesus, who has been taken up from you into heaven, will come in just the same way as you have watched Him go into heaven" (Acts 1:11; cp. Luke 24:51). As Peter later states, "Jesus . . . is at the right hand of God, having gone into heaven" (1 Pet 3:22).

Consequently, the Bible teaches that heaven is a place. Indeed, Jesus enters into heaven in a resurrected, material body (Luke 24:39; John 20:27). This shows clearly that heaven is a place rather than a state of mind, it is a real place rather than a symbol for our release from the sufferings of life. For this reason, Jesus encourages his disciples by saying: "In My Father's house are many dwelling places; if it were not so, I would have told you; for I go to prepare a place for you" (John 14:2).

Admittedly, the Scriptures do not teach us very much about what it is *like* in heaven, even though it teaches us about the *fact* of heaven. We do know that it is a place of rest (rather than burdensome toil), because Revelation 14:13 issues the following benediction: "'Blessed are the dead who die in the Lord from now on!' 'Yes,' says the Spirit, 'so that they may rest from their labors, for their deeds follow with them.'" And Hebrews 4:9 promises that "there remains a Sabbath rest for the people of God."

It also is a place of worship, for the highest angels themselves ceaselessly praise God: "day and night they do not cease to say, 'Holy, holy, holy is the Lord God, the Almighty, / Who was and Who is and Who is to come'" (Rev 4:8; cp. Isa 6:3). In fact, in Revelation John even provides us insight into the heavenly worship by the saints, as they unite their voices with the angels of God (Rev 4:11; 11:16; 19:4, 10; 22:8–9).

Heaven is a place of the highest bliss for the saved. Yet the Bible teaches that we will receive "rewards" in heaven based on our faithful labors on earth. Jesus' Parable of the Talents shows varying levels of blessing that await us (Luke 19:11–19).[5] Paul teaches this also in 1 Corinthians 3:8: "each will receive his own reward according to his own labor" (Rom 2:6). And John speaks of receiving "a full reward" (2 Jn 8).

Perhaps we find the most powerful statements in this direction in Paul and John. In 2 Corinthians 5:10 we read: "we must all appear before the judgment seat of Christ, so that each one may be recompensed for his deeds in the body, according to what he has done, whether good or bad." In Revelation 20:12 we read of the judgment even of those who names are found in the Book of Life:

> "I saw the dead, the great and the small, standing before the throne, and books were opened; and another book was opened, which is the book of life; and the dead were judged from the things which were written in the books, according to their deeds."

This rewarding of the righteous "according to their deeds," does not imply any sort of spiritual misery or tragic loss for those with lesser rewards. Heaven is a place of perfect blessing. Rather, this probably indicates that upon entering into one's final estate, the faithful Christian will enjoy a greater initial appreciation of the blessedness of salvation. That is, the reward is almost certainly in the subjective realm rather than in one's objective circumstances.

Perhaps we could liken the difference in reward by an illustration from human experience: If someone gives a $100 bill to an adult, he will appreciate it much more than if he gives it to a one year old. And this would be due to the greater level of maturity and understanding. Likewise we might expect those who grow in grace more on earth to appreciate more deeply the glory of heaven.

We enter heaven immediately upon death, not after a long period of "soul sleep," nor after being refined in "purgatory." Jesus informs the faithful thief on the cross: "Truly I say to you, today you shall be with Me in Paradise" (Luke 23:43). In Luke 16 Jesus' parable of the rich man and Lazarus shows that Lazarus enters heaven (under the image of "Abraham's bosom") while the rich man's brothers remain on earth under the possibility of conversion: "In Hades he lifted up his eyes, being in

---

[5] The "worthless slave" (Luke 19:22) is not a picture of a saved individual in heaven, but a lost person judged on the Day of Judgment (Luke 19:20–24, see especially v 27).

torment, and saw Abraham far away and Lazarus in his bosom" (Luke 16:23). Then he asks: "'Then I beg you, father, that you send him to my father's house — for I have five brothers — in order that he may warn them, so that they will not also come to this place of torment.' But Abraham said, 'They have Moses and the Prophets; let them hear them'" (Luke 16:27–29).

In two important texts, Paul specifically promises our immediate entry in to heaven. In 2 Corinthians 5:8 we read that as Christians we "prefer rather to be absent from the body and to be at home with the Lord." In Philippians 1:23–24 he states: "I am hard-pressed from both directions, having the desire to depart and be with Christ, for that is very much better; yet to remain on in the flesh is more necessary for your sake."

But now we must note that we have a glorious destiny even beyond heaven itself. So let us focus on:

Our Eternal Condition

The immediate entrance of our souls into heaven upon departing this life is a glorious expectation. But heaven is not our final destiny. God has more in store for us in the new, renovated earth which he will establish after the Final Judgment.

Scripture teaches that we may expect a reconstituted, material new earth for a variety of reasons. Consider the following evidence in this direction.

First, the biblical analogy. We may expect a renewed earth on the analogy of the transformation of the individual's body in the resurrection. When Jesus returns he will resurrect the dead into material bodies. Paul teaches that Christ's own resurrection is the "first fruits" of the full resurrection at the end. So then, whatever Christ's body is like at his resurrection is a sample of our resurrection bodies (1 Cor 15:20). In Philippians 3:21 we read that Jesus "will transform the body of our humble state into conformity with the body of His glory, by the exertion of the power that He has even to subject all things to Himself."

We know that Jesus dies in his physical body then comes back to life from the tomb (John 20:1–9). Jesus proves to doubting Thomas that his resurrected body is material: "Then He said to Thomas, 'Reach here with your finger, and see My hands; and reach here your hand and put it into My side; and do not be unbelieving, but believing'" (John 20:27). Later he presents himself to the disciples who are surprised when he approaches them: "'See My hands and My feet, that it is I Myself; touch Me and see, for a spirit does not have flesh and bones as you see that I have.' And when He had said this, He showed them His hands and His feet'" (Luke 24:39–40).

Thus, the Bible clearly teaches that we will receive a renewed physical body at the resurrection. And so, just as we receive a new body at the resurrection, so we will inherit a renewed earth on which to dwell with that body. As Paul teaches us:

> "For the earnest expectation of the creation eagerly waits for the revealing of the sons of God. For the creation was subjected to futility, not willingly, but because of Him who subjected it in hope; because the creation itself also will be delivered from the bondage of corruption into the glorious liberty of the children of God. For we know that the whole creation groans and labors with birth pangs together until now. And not only they, but we also who have the first fruits of the Spirit, even we ourselves groan within ourselves, eagerly waiting for the adoption, the redemption [resurrection] of our body." (Rom 8:19–23)

The comprehensive nature of sin and redemption (involving both soul and body), demands a comprehensive new earth (involving both spiritual and material aspects). Why else would we return to our physical bodies by means of resurrection, if we are to remain solely and forever in the spiritual, heavenly realm?

Indeed, we know that even the unbeliever will undergo a resurrection so as to endure a fuller judgment. Jesus warns his followers: "Do not fear those who kill the body but are unable to kill the soul; but rather fear Him who is able to destroy both soul and body in hell" (Matt 10:28).

Second, the biblical calling. Scripture seems to present our temporal labor in the physical earth as a training ground for eternity. As we strive to subdue the earth in a holy and spiritual fashion we are living up to God's design for us (Gen 1:26–28; Psa 8:5–8). In addition, our present cultural labors are clothed with eternal significance in that Scripture commands us in light of Christ's bodily resurrection to "be steadfast, immovable, always abounding in the work of the Lord, knowing that your labor is not in vain in the Lord" (1 Cor 15:58).

Theologian Anthony Hoekema explains: "We may firmly believe that products of science and culture produced by unbelievers may yet be found on the new earth. . . . Our mission work, our attempt to further a distinctively Christian culture, will have value not only for this world but even the world to come."[6] This comports well with the biblical calling to cultural and spiritual activity by the redeemed, who are images of God renewed by grace.

Third, the biblical assertion. We find the key passage presenting the consummate new heavens and new earth in 2 Peter 3:10–12:

> "The day of the Lord will come like a thief, in which the heavens will pass away with a roar and the elements will be destroyed with intense heat, and the earth and its works will be burned up. Since all these things are to be destroyed in this way, what sort of people ought you to be in holy conduct and godliness, looking for and hastening the coming of the day of God, because of which the heavens will be destroyed by burning, and the elements will melt with intense heat!"

This text points to the final, eternal order which follows the resurrection and the final judgment. Peter is not presenting us with the spiritual transformation that results from the gospel and is already occurring in history (2 Cor 5:17; Gal 6:15). In fact, the current spiritual realities themselves point to a final physical reality — much like our current spiritual resurrection in Christ (Eph 2:6; 1 John 3:14) points to the future physical resurrection at the end of history (John 5:24–29). Note the following arguments.

(1) Peter's whole thrust in his second epistle promotes a spiritual *perseverance* for the historical long run. That is, he writes about a long period in history that finally ends up in the eternal new creation. We see this in his urging his readers to persevere (2 Pet 1:6) and warning against short-sightedness (1:9). He states that Christians may have access to the eternal kingdom of Jesus Christ only through long-term perseverance (1:10–11, 19).

In fact, he does this by presenting Noah and Lot as examples of saints who persevere through evil times (like the evil times his faithful readers are facing). By persevering against their ungodly cultures, Noah and Lot come out on the other end of God's judgment *still upon the earth* (2 Pet 2:5, 7, 9). So Peter's readers should expect to come out on the other end

---

[6] Anthony Hoekema, *The Bible and the Future* (Grand Rapids: Eerdmans, 1979), 39–40.

of the chaos surrounding them (2:9a) — still on the earth because of God's power to deliver. God delivers Noah and Lot so that his name will continue on earth through their witness (2:6b; cp. 1:8) and offspring (2:5b) to live into the distant future.

Thus, those first-century Christians should expect their offspring to continue into the distant future (cp. 2 Pet 1:15). They must persevere even against false teachers who will arise among them (2:1). He is urging the Christians toward a long term commitment, not a short-term expectation. So then, while contemplating God's judgment cleansing of the earth in Noah's day (3:6), Peter urges Christians to many "holy livings" and "pieties" (*en hagiais anastrophais kai eusebeiais*, 3:11). These Greek plurals occur only here in Scripture. They suggest many acts of righteousness over the historical long term. Consequently, the epistle also ends with a call to perseverance (3:15, 17), just as it opens with such (1:6, 9). He calls on them to glorify Christ now and until "the day of eternity" (*eis hēmeran aiōnos*) begins — whenever that may be (3:18).

(2) Peter's audience (including us!) should expect mockers who scoff at Christ's promised second advent due to the long wait associated with it (2 Pet 3:3–4, 9). This waiting continues to our very day, and thus is truly long. Despite the trials coming soon (2:9), Peter warns that it may be thousands of years before Christ's return: "But, beloved, do not forget this one thing, that with the Lord one day is as a thousand years, and a thousand years as one day" (3:8).

(3) The Lord's longsuffering is due to a process that will take a long time. Nevertheless, they must understand that despite the long delay: "The Lord is not slack concerning His promise, as some count *slackness* [*braduteta*], but is *longsuffering* [*makrothumei*] toward us, not willing that any should perish but that all should come to repentance" (2 Pet 3:9 NKJV). They must "account that the *longsuffering* [*makrathumian*] of our Lord is salvation" (3:15a). This process of calling "all" to "repentance" spans the entire inter-adventual era and is still continuing to our very day. This "slowness" (*bradutēs*, v 9) of Christ's second advent allows the kingdom to continue to grow unto full fruition. This comports well with the slow growth of the kingdom like a mustard seed (Mt 13:31–32) and with the necessity of "all the days [*pasas tas hēmeras*]" for accomplishing the Great Commission (Mt 28:20).

(4) The destruction of the heavens and the earth that he envisions involves the current material creation. Peter expressly refers to the mater-

ial creation order: "from the beginning of creation" (2 Pet 3:4; cf. Gen 1:1); "by the word of God the heavens were of old, and the earth standing out of water and in the water" (3:5; cf. Gen 1:2, 9); "the heavens and the earth which now exist" (3:7). Thus, he defines the "heavens and earth" to which he refers and which God will replace with a "new heaven and a new earth" (3:10, 13). He is expecting the renovated, material new heavens and new earth at the second advent.

In conjunction with "the promise" of Christ's coming (2 Pet 3:4, 9), we will enter the ultimate "new heavens and new earth" (3:13). Here Peter is obviously borrowing terminology from Isaiah 65:17 (which speaks of a spiritual reality[7]). Yet as an inspired apostle he expands on that truth, looking to the ultimate outcome of the *spiritual* new heavens and earth in an *eternal* new heavens and earth.

The new creation, then, is the renovated material world that will succeed the present temporal order. God will purify and refashion it by fire. On this new earth the resurrected saints will dwell forever, engaging their activities and labors without the constraints of indwelling sin, a fallen environment, and the resistance of Satan and unbelievers.

Conclusion

The biblical doctrine of salvation holds forth glorious prospects for the believer. We learn in Scripture that God's blessings on us begin in the present, where he calls us to serve him in all of our labors. He even promises us that our labor will be fruitful and that we will be instruments of God in promoting and expanding his kingdom on earth.[8]

But our hope does not end with a job well done on earth. Upon our death we leave this world and enter into heaven where we will gather with the saints of old to worship and serve God in that glorious environment.

Yet neither is heaven our final resting place. God creates us as material creatures and will resurrect us in material bodies. And he does so in preparation for our inhabiting a renewed material creation: the consummate new heavens and the new earth.

---

[7] Isaiah is clearly speaking of the spiritual new heavens and new earth, not the consummate, physical new creation. After all, he mentions infants, aging, death, and curse in that prophecy (Isa 65:20).

[8] For more on this remarkable truth, see ch. 12 below.

The Truth about Salvation

REVIEW QUESTIONS FOR DISCUSSION

These questions deal directly with the material in this chapter. The answers can be found in the chapter.

1. How does the doctrine of creation impact our understanding of the doctrine of salvation?
2. What are "creation ordinances"? What are the three creation ordinances?
3. How are the "gospel" and the "kingdom of God" related?
4. What can we expect for the long-term for Christianity? Give evidence for your answer.
5. What is a fundamental difference between how the Christian understands man and how the secularist does?
6. What is the most fundamental significance of heaven?
7. Is heaven a place, or a state of mind? Give evidence for your answer.
8. What are some things we will do in heaven?
9. What do we mean by "rewards" at Judgment Day? How do we explain this in terms of heaven as a place of glorious bliss for all God's people?
10. List three biblical arguments that demand a new, material, reconstituted earth as our eternal abode.

STRETCHING FURTHER

These questions are designed to promote further group reflection on the topic beyond that which is presented in the chapter above.

1. What do we mean by the doctrine of "calling"?
2. What do we mean by a "worldview"?
3. Why do Christians have to stand before the Judgment Seat of Christ?
4. Why do you think the Bible does not tell us all that much about heaven?
5. Is Christ in heaven in his resurrected body now? How do you account for this?

Chapter 11
CHRISTIANS HAVE AN EVANGELISTIC OBLIGATION

As born-again believers in Christ we rejoice in *The Truth about Salvation*. Indeed, we are eternally grateful to God who saves us by his grace.

In our study we have seen that Christ promises that his kingdom will grow in the world, as a mustard seed grows to become a great plant (Matt 13:31–32). He even promises that after he dies he "will draw all men to myself" (John 12:32). On this basis he commands us to "make disciples of all the nations" (Matt 28:19). Therefore Paul declares that "God was in Christ reconciling the world to Himself" (2 Cor 5:19).

But now: how do unbelievers come to know about Christ and his saving love? How are they to find their way to his kingdom? They hear about salvation by means of what we call "evangelism."

Let us begin studying our evangelistic obligation by presenting:

The Definition of Evangelism

The word "evangelism" is derives from Greek, arising from either the noun *euangelion* or the verb *euangelizō*. This word is a compound word made from uniting the adverb *eu* ("good, beneficial") and the noun *angelia* ("message"). Thus, it basically means "good news."

In the New Testament the verb *euangelizō* appears fifty-four times. It can be translated as "proclaim the good news" or "preach the gospel" (e.g., Luke 1:19; 2:10; Acts 8:12; Rom 1:15; 1 Cor 9:16–18; Gal 1:8–9; Heb 4:2; etc.). The noun *euangelion* appears seventy-six times in the New Testament. It is translated either "good news" or "gospel" (Matt 4:23; 9:35; 24:14; Mark 1:14; Acts 15:7; Rom 1:1; 1 Cor 4:15; etc.).

Originally the Greek word *euangelion* spoke of the reward given to a messenger who brought the good news of a victory in battle or a deliverance from some disaster. In the New Testament it can refer to good news or encouraging information (Luke 1:19; 2:10; 1 Thess 3:6). But it generally refers to the good news of God's mercy in providing salvation for sinners, what we call the "gospel" (Mark 1:15; Rom 1:16; 1 Cor 4:15; etc.).[1]

Today we use the English word "evangelism" to refer to any activity that presents the gospel to sinners. Evangelism presents the gospel message, while warning sinners of the consequences of their current standing before God, explaining the way to gain salvation, and urging them to receive salvation by trusting in Christ.

But now let us consider more closely:

The Message of Evangelism

The fundamental message presented in evangelism is three-fold: (1) man is a sinner; (2) Christ is a Savior; and (3) God offers salvation to sinners. Let us briefly consider each one of these points in the evangelistic message.

First, man is a sinner deserving God's wrath. As a fallen sinner man stands in desperate need of salvation by a holy God. In chapter 2 above we studied our sinful condition, noting that man is legally fallen in Adam (Rom 5:12) and inherits Adam's sin nature through natural generation (Eph 2:3). Because of this he is therefore sinful in every facet of his being (Rom 1:28–31).

Thus, the Bible paints a bleak picture of man's condition outside of Christ. He is "dead in trespasses and sins' (Eph 2:1; cp. Col 2:13),"having no hope and without God in the world" (Eph 2:12), "darkened in their understanding" (Eph 4:18; cp. Rom 1:21), in "the snare of the devil, having been held captive by him to do his will" (2 Tim 2:26), and "helpless" (Rom 5:6). Consequently, "the wrath of God abides on him" (John 3:36) .

But, second, God sends his Son to save us from our sins. The gospel message is literally "good news" of the highest order — good news of eternal significance. Our God is holy and cannot simply overlook or dismiss sin without dealing with it, for "the LORD will by no means leave the guilty unpunished" (Nah 1:3).

Yet the gospel informs us that "God so loved the world, that He gave His only begotten Son, that whoever believes in Him shall not perish, but have eternal life" (John 3:16). Indeed, "when the fullness of the time

---

[1] Our English word "gospel" is from the Old English "god" (which means "good") and "spel" (which means message).

came, God sent forth His Son, born of a woman, born under the Law, so that He might redeem those who were under the Law, that we might receive the adoption as sons" (Gal 4:4–5).

So then the good news of the gospel is that God himself deals dramatically with the sin problem: he sends his Son to stand in the place of the sinner so that he might endure God's holy wrath against sin. Paul puts the matter thus: "while we were still helpless, at the right time Christ died for the ungodly" so that he "demonstrates His own love toward us, in that while we were yet sinners, Christ died for us" (Rom 5:6, 8). Paul even teaches that this is taught throughout the Scriptures and is of fundamental significance: "I delivered to you as of first importance what I also received, that Christ died for our sins according to the Scriptures, and that He was buried, and that He was raised on the third day according to the Scriptures" (1 Cor 15:3–4).

The New Testament employs a powerful technical term to relate the means whereby God forgives us through Christ's redemptive work: "propitiation" (Greek: *hilasmos*). We see this term in four New Testament passages: Romans 3:25; Hebrews 2:17; 1 John 2:2; 4:10. This word is more powerful than "expiation," with which it is often confused. Expiation speaks of the cancellation of sin by forgiving. But propitiation speaks of the forgiveness of sin by turning away God's wrath — and in the New Testament this turning away of God's wrath is by Christ's absorbing it in himself.

We see this clearly exhibited in Romans 3:25 where we read of Jesus Christ "whom God displayed publicly as a propitiation in His blood through faith. This was to demonstrate His righteousness, because in the forbearance of God He passed over the sins previously committed." That the propitiating forgiveness comes through Christ's "blood" indicates that it is secured by his death under God's wrath. As the perfect and holy Son of God, he alone can pay the sin debt. And he does this by personally enduring God's wrath in our place. Thus, "having now been justified by His blood, we shall be saved from the wrath of God through Him" (Rom 5:9; cp. 1 Thess 1:10).

Thus, God "made Him who knew no sin to be sin on our behalf, so that we might become the righteousness of God in Him" (2 Cor 5:21). By his propitiating work, "Christ redeemed us from the curse of the Law, having become a curse for us" (Gal 3:13).

Third, God offers salvation freely to all who would receive it. In the gospel message God offers salvation from sin through Jesus Christ. Though only the elect will believe the gospel and be saved (John 6:37, 39; 17:2, 24; Acts 13:48), the offer of salvation is full and free.

As God proclaims through Isaiah: "Ho! Every one who thirsts, come to the waters; / And you who have no money come, buy and eat. / Come, buy wine and milk / Without money and without cost" (Isa 55:1). Revelation speaks of the free offer of the gospel by alluding to Isaiah 55:1: "the Spirit and the bride say, 'Come.' And let the one who hears say, 'Come.' And let the one who is thirsty come; let the one who wishes take the water of life without cost" (Rev 22:17). And Jesus reflects this truth when he preaches: "come to Me, all who are weary and heavy-laden, and I will give you rest" (Matt 11:28).

God is a gracious God who even "causes His sun to rise on the evil and the good, and sends rain on the righteous and the unrighteous" (Matt 5:45). Because he is a merciful God he declares: "'As I live!' declares the Lord GOD, 'I take no pleasure in the death of the wicked, but rather that the wicked turn from his way and live'" (Eze 33:11).

Therefore, in the New Testament we see the message of salvation proclaimed to all. Just before his ascension, Jesus instructs his disciples "that repentance for forgiveness of sins would be proclaimed in His name to all the nations" (Luke 24:27). Paul busies himself with this universal message: "God is now declaring to men that all people everywhere should repent" (Acts 17:30).

Since man cannot save himself, salvation does not come through the sinner's work. Rather God offers salvation through Christ to those who will receive it by faith. Perhaps no verse in the Bible captures the essence of God's gracious message of salvation as well as Ephesians 2:8–9: "For by grace you have been saved through faith; and that not of yourselves, it is the gift of God; not as a result of works, so that no one may boast" (cp. 2 Tim 1:9; Tit 3:5).

We see Peter proclaiming the gospel message along these lines when he preaches: "of Him [Christ] all the prophets bear witness that through His name everyone who believes in Him receives forgiveness of sins" (Acts 10:43; cp. Acts 13:39). Therefore, we who would undertake the work of evangelism must present the gospel as does Paul: "believe in the Lord Jesus, and you will be saved" (Acts 16:31).

As we saw in chapter 9, though, true faith is deeper than merely assenting to the truth. After all, "the demons also believe, and shudder" (Jms 2:18). Rather it involves a deep, personal commitment to Christ. In fact, faith is the positive aspect of the sinner's response which is necessarily linked to the negative aspect: repentance.

As we noted in chapter 7 repentance and faith are inextricably linked in true conversions. This is why Paul can explain his ministry by noting that he testifies "of repentance toward God and faith in our Lord Jesus Christ" (Acts 20:21). Repentance is "from dead works" whereas "faith [is] toward God" (Heb 6:1).

Not surprisingly, then, we see calls to repent in numerous passages, including Matt 3:2; 4:17; Luke 5:32; 13:3; 15:10; Acts 2:38; 3:19; 5:31; 17:30; 2 Tim 2:25, to name but a few. Jesus even summarizes his gospel message when he declares to his disciples "that repentance for forgiveness of sins would be proclaimed in His name to all the nations" (Luke 24:47).

But now let us consider:

The Necessity of Evangelism

Sinners outside of Christ are lost and under the threat of God's eternal wrath. And though salvation comes through the instrumentality faith, they cannot even believe in him on their own. This is because they are spiritually dead (Eph 2:1; Col 2:15) — which explains why the New Testament speaks of salvation as being "born again" (John 3:3, 7; 1 Pet 1:3, 23), passing from death to life (John 5:24; 1 John 3:14), and being made alive in Christ (Rom 6:11; Eph 2:1, 5).

Because of the sinner's spiritual deadness, God has to give them faith (i.e., the capacity and will to believe). In this regard Paul specifically states that "by grace you have been saved through faith; and *that* not of yourselves, it [faith] is the gift of God" (Eph 2:8). As he says elsewhere: "to you it has been *granted* for Christ's sake . . . to believe in Him" (Phil 1:29). He even desires regarding unbelievers that "God may *grant* them repentance leading to the knowledge of the truth" (2 Tim 2:25). Truly in salvation God works within "both to will and work for His good pleasure" (Phil 2:13).

As Jesus explains man's problem: "no one can [Greek: *dunamai*] come to Me unless the Father who sent Me draws him" (John 6:44). According to the Danker lexicon, the Greek word *dunamai* means "to possess capability . . . *can, am able, be capable*."² For instance, in John 3:4 Nicodemus uses this word two times in his question to Christ: "How *can* [*dunamai*] a man be born when he is old? He cannot [*dunamai*] enter a second time into his mother's womb and be born, can he?"

The Lord mentions this problem again when he asks those who are resisting his message: "why do you not understand what I am saying? It is because you cannot [*dunamai*] hear My word" (John 8:43). Again, sinners do not have the capability to believe in Christ in themselves. Paul teaches this as well, noting that the "natural man does not accept the things of the Spirit of God, for they are foolishness to him; and he cannot [*dunamai*] understand them, because they are spiritually appraised" (1 Cor 2:14).

It is true that as creatures made in the image of God (Gen 1:26–27; 9:6), all men know him deep down within. Indeed, Paul teaches that "that which is known about God is evident within them; for God made it evident to them" (Rom 1:19; cp. Acts 14:17). Yet this innate knowledge of God is not a saving knowledge of God and does not even help them turn to him, for their sin is such that they "suppress the truth in unrighteousness" (Rom 1:18).

Consequently, Christians must take the good news of salvation to the sinner. In Romans Paul writes: "whoever will call on the name of the Lord will be saved. How then will they call on Him in whom they have not believed? How will they believe in Him whom they have not heard? And how will they hear without a preacher?" (Rom 10:13–14).

This is why Jesus states that "repentance for forgiveness of sins" must "be proclaimed in His name to all the nations" (Luke 24:47). This is why he commands that we are to "go therefore and make disciples of all the nations" (Matt 28:19). This is why Paul cites Isaiah 49:6 to explain his calling to preach the gospel: "the Lord has commanded us, 'I have placed you as a light for the Gentiles, that you may bring salvation to the end of the earth'" (Acts 13:47).

The Obligation to Evangelism

There are many reasons why we should engage in evangelism. We will list several that should encourage us to "do the work of an evangelist" (2 Tim 4:5).

---

² Frederick William Danker, *A Greek-English Lexicon of the New Testament and Other Early Christian Literature* (Chicago: University Press, 200), 262

First, we should evangelize out of obedience to Christ. The Lord tells us that he came to "seek and to save that which was lost" (Luke 19:10). Paul states that Jesus "came into the world to save sinners" (1 Tim 1:15). Christ begins that work during his earthly ministry then commands us to continue it: "go therefore and make disciples of all the nations, baptizing them in the name of the Father and the Son and the Holy Spirit" (Matt 28:19).

In fact, Paul states that "God was in Christ reconciling the world to Himself, not counting their trespasses against them, and He has committed to us the word of reconciliation" (2 Cor 5:19). Since he has committed the word of reconciliation to us, we must obey his commission.

Second, we should evangelize to glorify God. Of course, everything we do should be done to God's glory (1 Cor 10:31). But promoting God's saving word to sinners in the world is a special way to glorify God. Jesus teaches his followers in the Sermon on the Mount:

> "You are the light of the world. A city set on a hill cannot be hidden; nor does anyone light a lamp and put it under a basket, but on the lampstand, and it gives light to all who are in the house. Let your light shine before men in such a way that they may see your good works, and glorify your Father who is in heaven." (Matt 5:14–17)

God is glorified in the salvation of sinners. Paul repeatedly emphasizes this in his letter to the Ephesians. When we are adopted as sons through Christ it is "the praise of the glory of His grace" (Eph 1:5–6). The goal of our salvation is "to the praise of His glory" (Eph 1:12). Our final redemption in heaven is "to the praise of His glory" (Eph 1:14). As salvation spreads great glory abounds to God: "the grace which is spreading to more and more people may cause the giving of thanks to abound to the glory of God" (2 Cor 4:15).

Third, we should evangelize out of compassion for sinners. Proverbs 24:11 commands: "deliver those who are being taken away to death, / And those who are staggering to slaughter." Jude urges: "save others, snatching them out of the fire; and on some have mercy with fear, hating even the garment polluted by the flesh" (Jude 23). Paul's testimony should be ours: "knowing the fear of the Lord, we persuade men" (2 Cor 5:11).

Fourth, we should evangelize to be free from the blood of men. Jesus alerts his disciples to the dire predicament of sinners, stating that "the gate is wide and the way is broad that leads to destruction, and there are many who enter through it" (Matt 7:13). Thus, sinners desperately need the gospel of Christ that we as Christians have.

When Paul left the church at Ephesus, he could declare: "I know that all of you, among whom I went about preaching the kingdom, will no longer see my face. Therefore, I testify to you this day that I am innocent of the blood of all men. For I did not shrink from declaring to you the whole purpose of God" (Acts 20:25–27). This concept of spiritual responsibility appears in God's appointment of Ezekiel to declare his will:

"Son of man, I have appointed you a watchman to the house of Israel; whenever you hear a word from My mouth, warn them from Me. When I say to the wicked, 'You will surely die,' and you do not warn him or speak out to warn the wicked from his wicked way that he may live, that wicked man shall die in his iniquity, but his blood I will require at your hand." (Eze 3:17–18)

These should be four compelling reasons to proclaim the gospel to the lost. We could list others, but these clearly underscore the Christian responsibility to spread the gospel of Jesus Christ.

Conclusion

In America and generally in the West we live in a culture that has historically been strongly impacted by Christianity. This means that when you speak to people about Christ, they will at least know generally what you are talking about. But it also means they may well think they are already Christians because they have a superficial knowledge of Christianity. This will add to the challenge of presenting the gospel compelling.

But we all know that Christian influence is declining all around us. This means that our once-Christian culture needs the gospel. You must understand, though, that the gospel that saved you from your sins has the same power to save every other person. You must not be fearful of proclaiming the gospel. Paul greatly encourages us when he states that "the gospel is the power of God for salvation" (Rom 1:16).

To encourage you in your confidence in the gospel, the next chapter will be dealing with the absolute certainty of the Christian faith.

REVIEW QUESTIONS FOR DISCUSSION

These questions deal directly with the material in this chapter. The answers can be found in the chapter.

1. How would you define "evangelism"?
2. What is the significance of the Greek word translated "gospel"?
3. What are the three basic elements in the evangelistic message?
4. Where do we find in the Bible our obligation to engage in evangelism?
5. Why does man have to have some understanding of sin and his sinfulness before he will truly believe in Christ?
6. What does the word "propitiation" mean? Why do we say it is such a strong word for salvation?
7. Why is evangelism necessary?
8. What are some reasons why we should should engage in evangelism?
9. How is God glorified in the sinner's salvation?
10. You have engaged such a good study that you will not have to answer ten questions, but will get time off for good behavior. Instead, you will receive a free joke: A little girl was drawing a picture in school when the teacher came by and asked her what she was drawing. She explained: "Jonah getting swallowed by a whale." The teacher replied: "That didn't really happen. Jonah would have been killed." The little girl declared in frustration: "I know he did! When I get to heaven, I'm going to ask him if he was swallowed by a whale!" To this the teacher responded: "What if he didn't go to heaven?" The little girl took up the challenge and stated: "Well, in that case *you* ask him!"

STRETCHING FURTHER

These questions are designed to promote further group reflection on the topic beyond that which is presented in the chapter above.

1. How did you become a Christian? By evangelistic outreach? Or by family nurturing in the faith?
2. Have you ever led anyone to a saving knowledge of Christ?

3. Christ says that loving your neighbor as yourself is one of the two great commandments (Matt 22:39–40). How does this impact your obligation to evangelism?
4. What does Jesus mean when he commands us to "make disciples" of all the nations? What is discipleship?
5. How is it that we are responsible for evangelizing sinners, if it is God who actually saves them by his sovereign action?

Chapter 12
CHRISTIANITY IS A CERTAIN FAITH

The Truth about Salvation is: we are saved by the grace of God who redeems us from all our sin. As Paul puts it: "He rescued us from the domain of darkness, and transferred us to the kingdom of His beloved Son, in whom we have redemption, the forgiveness of sins" (Col 1:13–14).

In this final chapter of our study of *The Truth about Salvation* we will focus on the certainty of the Christian faith. Our holy faith is not just an empty, wishful matter of the heart, as the secularists believe it to be. Rather Christianity is a certain faith that provides the only rational foundation for all of life, as we will see.

The certainty of our faith has a two-fold, direct relevance to *The Truth about Salvation*: (1) It comforts us in our holy faith to know that we are committed to the absolute truth. (2) It encourages us in our evangelistic outreach to know that we have the answers to man's deepest questions and most earnest longings.

God calls upon those saved by his grace to "sanctify Christ as Lord in your hearts, always being ready to make a defense to everyone who asks you to give an account for the hope that is in you, yet with gentleness and reverence" (1 Pet 3:15). As we obey him we must defend the faith in such a way that it "sanctifies the Lord" in our hearts. We must defend the faith from a position of faith. Too many defenses of the faith cede the method of approach to the unbeliever and end up "proving" at best the *possibility* that *a god* exists — not the certainty that the God of Scripture exists.

Let us see how we may do this.

Rational Thought and Presuppositions

Before we can establish the certainty of the Christian faith, we must begin by noting the nature of reality as created by God. We will begin by presenting:

Uniformity in Nature

We exist in what is known as a "universe." The word "universe" is derived from the Latin *universum*. This Latin word is a compound of two parts: *unus*, meaning "one" (as in "unit") and *vertere*, meaning "turn." It literally means "all turned into one, all together." This word speaks of all created things regarded collectively.

Thus, the word "universe" indicates that we live in a *single* unified, orderly, coherent system which is composed of many diversified parts. These parts function coordinately together as a whole, rational system. We do not live in a "*multi*verse." A multiverse state-of-affairs would be a dis-unified, totally fragmented, and random assortment of disconnected and un*connectable* facts. These unconnectable facts would be meaninglessly scattered about in chaotic disarray and ultimate disorder.

The concept of a *uni*verse is vitally important to science. For the very possibility of scientific investigation wholly depends on the fact of a "universe"— an orderly, rational coherent, unified system. If reality were haphazard and disorderly we could have no basic scientific laws that govern and control the various phenomena of reality. And if this were the case, there would be no unity at all in either reality itself, or in experience, or in thought.

In such a multiverse each and every single fact would necessarily stand alone, utterly disconnected from other facts, not forming a system as a whole. Consequently, nothing could be organized and related in a mind because no fact would be related to any other fact. Thus, science, logic, and experience are absolutely dependent upon uniformity as a principle of the natural world.

As we opened our study of *The Truth about Salvation* we began with the ultimate fact: our God is the Creator of all things. He is the one before whom all men must bow. And he reveals in Genesis 1 that he creates, structures, and upholds the rational universe. The God we trust for salvation is the God of creation; the God we present in evangelism is the God of all reality.

Uniformity and Faith

But now the question arises: How do we know assuredly that the universe is in fact uniform? Has man investigated every single aspect of the universe from each one of its smallest atomic particles to its farthest galaxy (which scientists have designated: z8_GND_5296).[1] And has he examined all that exists in between so that he can speak authoritatively and with absolute confidence?

Does man have totally exhaustive knowledge about every particle of matter, every movement in space, and every moment of time? How does man know uniformity governs the world and the universe?

Furthermore, how can we know that uniformity will continue tomorrow so that we can conjecture about future events? And since man claims to have an experience of external things, how do we know our experience is accurate and actually conforms to reality as it is?

Such questions are not commonly asked, but are nevertheless vitally important to consider. The point of these questions is to demonstrate a particular phenomenon: any and every attempt to prove uniformity in nature necessarily requires *circular reasoning*. To prove uniformity one must assume or presuppose uniformity.

If I set out to argue the uniformity of the universe because I can predict cause-and-effect, am I not presupposing the uniformity and validity of my experience? How can I be sure that my experience of cause-and-effect is an accurate reflection of what really happens? Furthermore, am I not presupposing the trustworthy, uniform coherence of my own rationality — a rationality that requires uniformity to begin with?

The issue boils down to this: Since man cannot know everything he must *assume* or *presuppose* uniformity and then think and act on this very basic assumption. *Consequently the principle of uniformity is not a scientific law but an act of faith which undergirds scientific* law. Thus, adherence to the principle of uniformity — though basic to science — is an intrinsically religious commitment. And as we shall see, only Christianity can account for it.

Presuppositions in Thought

Scientists follow a basic pattern in discovering true scientific laws. First, they observe a particular phenomenon. Then on the basis of their observations they construct a working hypothesis. Next, experiments are performed implementing this hypothesis. This is followed in turn by an

---

[1] Elizabeth Landau, "Scientists confirm most distant galaxy ever," *CNN Tech* (10/25/2013). http://www.cnn.com/2013/10/23/tech/innovation/most-distant-galaxy/

attempt to verify the experiments performed. Then a verified hypothesis is accepted as a theory. Finally a well-established theory is recognized as a scientific law which governs in a given set of circumstances.

Thus, the basic pattern of scientific activity is: observation, hypothesis, experimentation, verification, theory, and law. Christians agree whole-heartedly with the validity of this scientific methodology. We accept the notion of a uniform universe which allows for such, for "in the beginning God created the heavens and the earth" (Gen 1:1) and he "upholds all things by the word of His power" (Heb 1:3). .

Physicist Thomas Kuhn, in his epochal 1962 work titled The *Structure of Scientific Revolutions,* noted that scientists *must* work from certain preconceived ideas. That is, they must operate on the basis of certain presupposed ideas about things in order to begin formulating their theories and performing their experiments.

That presuppositions are always silently at work is evident in that when dealing with a particular problem scientists select only a few basic facts to consider while rejecting or overlooking numerous others. They perform certain types of experiments while neglecting others. And *they do this in keeping* with *their presuppositions.* One of the most basic presuppositions that scientists hold is the one we are considering: the universe is in fact one orderly, rational, coherent system. Were this not assumed then science could not even get off the ground.

But, as a matter of fact, all men hold to *numerous* presuppositions that play a vital role in all human thought and behavior. The various presuppositions we hold govern the way we think and act, all the way down to how we select and employ specific facts from the countless number presented to us each moment. Basic presuppositions are the foundation blocks upon which we build our way of understanding the world about us. Presuppositions are the very basis for what is known as our "world-and-life" view, more succinctly called a "worldview."

A worldview is the framework through which we understand the world and our relation to it. Everyone necessarily has a particular way of looking at the world which serves to organize ideas about the world in his mind. This worldview must be founded on basic presupposed ideas that we hold to be truth. We begin with certain presuppositions and build from there in our learning, communicating, behaving, planning, and so forth.

The Impossibility of Neutrality

Everyone holds to presuppositions. No one operates — or even *can* operate — from a vacuum. We simply do not think or behave "out of the blue." It is impossible to think and live as if we were aliens having just arrived in this world from a radically different universe, totally devoid of all knowledge of this world, absolutely objective and utterly un-predisposed to ideas about truth. Rather, people behave in terms of a basic worldview which implements their conceptions regarding truth.

Consequently, neutrality in thought is impossible. Each person — the philosopher and scientist included — has his own bias. This bias has predetermined the *facts* on the basis of his presuppositions. Yet almost invariably scientists claim to be presenting neutral, unbiased, impartial and objective facts in their research.

Unfortunately for this line of thinking, man is not and cannot be truly objective and impartial. *All thinking must begin somewhere!* All thinking must have some fundamental, logically primitive starting point or presupposition. At the very least we must presuppose the reality of the external world, the rationality of mental activity, the compatibility between external reality and the mind, and the uniformity of nature, i.e., the law of cause-and-effect. As noted previously a certain *faith* is necessary in the selection and organization of the several facts chosen from the innumerable number flowing toward us in every moment of experience.

By the very nature of the case *presuppositions are necessarily self-authenticating or self-evidencing*. That is, facts are inseparable from their interpretation. Facts *cannot* stand alone. They must be understood in terms of some broad, unified whole or system. They must be organized in our rational minds in terms of their general relationships to other facts and principles.

This leads us then to our most basic question: Which system of thought can give meaning to the facts of the universe? Which worldview can provide an adequate foundation for reality? Why is our state-of-affairs conducive to rational thought and behavior? What is the basis for an orderly universe?

Worldviews in Collision

When we contrast Christian thought with non-Christian thought we must realize that we are *not* contrasting two series of isolated facts. We are not comparing two systems of truth sharing a basically similar outlook with only intermittent differences at specific turns. *We are contrasting two whole, complete, and antithetical systems of thought.*

Each particular item of evidence presented in support of the one's system of belief will be evaluated by the other system. And it will be evaluated in terms of the latter's own entire implicit *system* with all of its basic assumptions. Each fact or piece of data presented either to the Christian or the non-Christian will be weighed, categorized, organized, and judged as to its possibility and significance in terms of the all pervasive worldview held.

Consequently, it is essential that we see the debate between the Christian and the non-Christian as a debate engaging two complete worldviews — as a debate between two ultimate commitments and presuppositions which are contrary to one another. Two complete philosophies are in collision. Appealing to various *scientific evidences* would be arbitrated *in terms of* the two mutually-exclusive and diametrically opposed, presupposed truths held by the systems.

Thus, the debate between the Christian and the non-Christian *must eventually work its way down to the question of one's ultimate authority.* Every series of arguments must end somewhere; one's conclusions could never be demonstrated if they were dependent upon an infinite regress of argumentation and justification. So all debates must terminate at *some* point, at some premise held as unquestionable. This is one's foundational starting point, one's ultimate authority or presupposition.

The question which now surfaces is: Which system of truth provides the foundational preconditions essential for observation, reason, experience, and meaningful discourse? Thus, which *faith* system should be chosen; the Christian or the non-Christian?

Christian Truth and Presuppositions

What is the Christian's starting point? What is his most basic presupposition upon which he builds his entire world view? Where do we begin our argument?

Christian thought holds as its logically primitive, fundamental, all-pervasive and necessary starting point or presupposition: the being of God who has revealed himself in Scripture. Thus, our presupposition is God and his Word. The Scripture, being his own infallible word (2 Tim 3:16), reveals to us the nature of the God in whom we trust. It reveals to us the God of our salvation, the God we promote in evangelism, the God who underlies *The Truth about Salvation*.

God is self-sufficient, needing nothing outside of himself at all (Exo 4:11; John 5:26). All else in the universe is utterly dependent upon him (Col 1:17; Heb 1:3). God is the all-powerful Creator of the entire universe (Gen 1:1; Exo 20:11; Neh 9:6).

Furthermore, God is personal, thus giving meaning to the vast universe (Acts 17:28). And he has clearly and authoritatively revealed himself in Scripture (2 Pet 1:20–21), so that we may build upon his Word as truth (Psa 119:160; John 17:17). The Word that we must proclaim in our evangelistic encounter, is the Word which undergirds all of reality.

The entire Christian system of thought is founded solidly upon this God; the all-ordering God of Scripture (Psa 33:9; Isa 46:10). We presuppose God for what he is. If God exists and demands our belief in Scripture, we cannot challenge or test him in any area (Deut 6:16; Matt 4:7). We recognize the independence of God, as well as the utter dependence of man and even of the universe. Thus we do not have to exhaustively know everything to be sure. God knows all things and has revealed to us in his Word the truth of uniformity (Gen 8:22; Col 1:17; Heb 1:3) and all other truths we need in order to build our lives upon.

Secular Thought and Presuppositions

Against this presupposed system, what does the non-Christian presuppose as ultimate truth? What does the secularist have to offer as its ultimate authority?

The non-Christian must ultimately explain the universe *not* on the basis of the all-organizing, self-sufficient, all-wise, personal God of Scripture as his starting point. Rather he must explain the universe by nebulous, chaotic, impersonal chance. He asserts that the universe was produced by a combination of impersonal chance plus an enormous span of time. Thus the ultimate starting point and the all-conditioning environment of the universe is time plus chance.

Because of the secularist's starting point, *rational* science is rooted in the *irrationality* of chance. The scientist cannot speak of design or purpose in the universe because there is neither a designer or a purpose. There can be no goal or purpose in a random system.

On this view science *must* by the very nature of its non-Christian commitment assume facts to be bits of irrationalism strewn about awaiting rationalization by man. Because of this, modem secular science is schizophrenic. On the one hand, everything has its source in random, ungoverned chance. On the other hand, evolution assumes all is not random, but uniform. It holds that all is ungoverned, yet, nevertheless, is moving in an upward direction from disorder to order, from simplicity to complexity.

In this regard Christian philosopher Cornelius Van Til has noted: "On his own assumption his own rationality is a product of chance. The rationality and purpose that he may be searching for are still bound by products of chance."[2] To prove a rational universe by chance man must believe the rational is the product of, and is dependent upon, the irrational. They must believe that rationality is rooted in irrationality.

In the non-Christian system all of reality founded on chance. Not only so, but this leaves man to be the final criterion of truth: Man — sinful, fallible, finite man — becomes ultimate in the non-Christian system.

Worldview Elements and Presuppositions

For a belief system to be a *world*view it must account for the most basic elements of the world and life. The four most basic features of a worldview is its view of reality (what philosophers call "ontology"), knowledge (technically known as "epistemology"), morality, and purpose ("teleology"). Christianity alone can rationally account for these essential worldview elements. The salvation we depend on is rooted in the all-ordering God of reality.

Reality (Ontology)

When asked to give the basis and starting point for the orderly universe and all external reality, the Christian points to the self-contained, omnipresent all-powerful, all-wise God of Scripture.

When the non-Christian is asked to give the basis and starting for the orderly universe and external reality, he points literally to nothing. All has risen from nothing by the irrational mechanism of chance.

---

[2] Cornelius Van Til, *The Defense of the Faith* (Phillipsburg, N.J.: P & R, 1955), 102

When asked if something can miraculously pop into being from nothing in an instant, the non-Christian vigorously responds in the negative. Instant miracles are out of the question! But when asked if something can come out of nothing *if given several billion years,* the non-Christian confidently responds in the affirmative. As Van Til has noted, the non-Christian overlooks the fact that if one zero equals zero, then a billion zeros can equal only zero.

Thus, the Christian has a *more than adequate reason* for the universe, whereas the non-Christian has *no reason whatsoever.* So then, *The Truth about Salvation* not only saves man's soul, but reality itself.

Knowledge (Epistemology)

The Christian establishes his theory of knowledge on the all-ordering, all-knowing God of Scripture. God has immediate, true, and exhaustive knowledge of everything. And he has revealed to man in the Bible comprehensive principles which are clear and provide a sure foundation for knowledge.

Such a foundation for knowledge insures that what man does know (although he cannot know all things) he can know truly. Knowledge does work because man's mind as created by God is receptive to external reality and is given validity by God Himself.

On the other hand, the non-Christian must establish his theory of knowledge on the same foundation upon which he established reality: nebulous chaos and irrational chance. If followed out consistently the non-Christian theory of knowledge would utterly destroy all knowledge, causing it to drown in the turbulent ocean of irrationalism. *There is no reason for reason in the non-Christian system.* The concepts of probability, possibility, order, rationality, and so forth, are impossible in a chance system.

Thus, the Christian has a sure foundation for knowledge, whereas the non-Christian has none. *The Truth about Salvation* not only saves man's soul, but the possibility of knowledge.

Morality (Ethics)

When we consider the issue of moral behavior — how we shall conduct ourselves in life — again the question must be settled in terms of one's system, one's worldview.

For the Christian, morality is founded upon the all-good, all-knowing, everywhere-present, all- powerful, personal, and eternal God of Scripture. His will, which is rooted in his being and nature, is man's standard of right. Since God is all good (Psa 119:137; Mark 10:18b) and all-knowing (Psa. 139:2–27; Prov. 15:3), moral principles revealed in Scripture are always relevant to our situation. Since God is eternal (Psa. 90:2; 102:12), his moral commands are *always* binding upon men.

For the non-Christian there is no sure base for ethics. Since reality is founded on nothing and knowledge is rooted in irrationalism, morality can be nothing other than pure, impersonal irrelevance. In such a system as presupposed by non-Christian thought there are no — *there can be no* — ultimate, abiding moral principles. Everything is caught up in the impersonal flux of a random universe. Random change is an ultimate in such a system, consequently ethics is reduced to pure relativism. Non-Christian thought can offer no justification for any moral behavior whatsoever.

The Truth about Salvation not only saves man's soul, but morality.

Purpose (Teleology)

To the question of whether or not the universe and life have *any* significance and meaning, the Christian confidently responds in the affirmative. There is meaning in the world because it was purposely *and* purposefully created by *and* for the personal, loving, all-ordering, eternal God of Scripture (Neh 9:6; Psa 33:6–9). Man came about as the direct and purposeful creation of a tender and loving God (Gen 2:7).

Furthermore, man was assigned a specific and far-reaching duty by God on the very day he was created (Gen 1:26-29). Man and *his task* must be understood *in terms* of the eternal God and his plan rather than in terms of himself and an environment of chance and change.

Non-Christian thought destroys the meaning and significance of man by positing that he is nothing more than a chance fluke, an accidental collection of molecules arising out of the slime of the primordial ooze. Man is a frail speck of dust caught up in a gigantic, impersonal, multi-billion year old universe. That, and nothing more. As the famous Twentieth Century atheist Bertrand Russell put it:

> "The world is purposeless, void of meaning. Man is the outcome of accidental collocations of atoms; all th devotion, all th inspiration, all the noonday brightness of human genius are destined to extinction in the vast death of the solar system. Only on the

firm foundation of unyielding despair can the soul's habitation be safely built. From evolution no ultimately optimistic philosophy can be validly inferred."[3]

The Truth about Salvation not only saves man's soul, but meaning and purpose in life.

Conclusion

To the question concerning which system is the most adequate for explaining external reality, the possibility of knowledge, a relevant and binding ethic, and the significance of man, the answer should be obvious. Actually the defense of Christianity is simple: we argue the impossibility of the contrary. By this we mean that the proof of the Christian faith is the impossibility of its non-existence. Without the Christian truth claims revealed in Scripture, we could not account for any of these key components of life.

Thus, those who assault the Christian system must actually *assume* it in order to do so. As strange as it may seem, atheism assumes theism. If the God of Scripture did not exist there would be no man in any real world to argue — there would be no possibility of rationality by which an argument could be forged, and there would be no purpose in debate!

Charles Darwin stated it well in his personal letter to W. Graham on July 3, 1881:

"But then with me the horrid doubt always arises whether the convictions of man's mind, which has always been developed from the mind of the lower animals, are of any value or at all trustworthy. Would any one trust in the convictions of a monkey's mind, if there are any convictions in such a mind?"[4]

Paul also spoke well when he declared in Romans 3:4, "Let God be true and every man a liar." And as he commands the Christian who knows *The Truth about Salvation*: "this I say, and affirm together with the Lord, that you walk no longer just as the Gentiles [unbelievers] also walk, in the futility of their mind, being darkened in their understanding, excluded

---

[3] Bertrand Russell, *Mysticism and Logic* (New York: Doubleday, 1917), 45–46.

[4] Francis Darwin, ed., *The Life and Letters of Charles Darwin* (New York: Basic, 1959), 1:285.

from the life of God because of the ignorance that is in them, because of the hardness of their heart" (Eph 4:17–18).

The God of Scripture, the Father of our Lord Jesus Christ, the Savior of God's elect, is the ultimate and necessary foundation for a rational, coherent worldview. Every other system is built upon a lie, upon futility. The Christian system begins with: "In the beginning God." And from that foundational reality, all the rest of a rational worldview falls into place.

REVIEW QUESTIONS FOR DISCUSSION

These questions deal directly with the material in this chapter. The answers can be found in the chapter.

1. Where in Scripture does God call us to engage in defending the faith?
2. How does the certainty of the Christian faith help us in our own lives and in promoting the gospel?
3. What do we mean by the "uniformity of nature?" How is it an important concept for science?
4. How is the uniformity of nature a function of faith? Explain.
5. What are presuppositions? Why are they important?
6. What do we mean by "the impossibility of neutrality"? How is this notion helpful for defending the faith?
7. What is the ultimate presupposition in the Christian faith?
8. How does the secular view of science actually undermine science? How does the Christian faith encourage it?
9. How does secularism undermine the possibility of knowledge? How does the Christian faith encourage it?
10. How does secularism undermine the possibility of morality? How does the Christian faith encourage it?

STRETCHING FURTHER

These questions are designed to promote further group reflection on the topic beyond that which is presented in the chapter above.

1. What is "apologetics"?
2. What are the leading schools of apologetics? Define each school in a few sentences.
3. Who are some leading Christian apologists in our day?
4. Have you ever read a book on apologetics or formally studied apologetics? Was it helpful?
5. Have you ever had someone challenge your Christian faith with: "How do you know for sure?" How would you respond?

CONCLUSION

No doctrine of Scripture is more important to us than the doctrine of salvation. This great doctrine brings us the marvelous news of acceptance with God in the present and the wonderful hope of salvation by God for eternity. Understanding *The Truth about Salvation* is a crucial matter for all men, so that they might answer Job's question: "How then can a man be just with God?" (Job 25:4).

As we have studied *The Truth about Salvation* we have focused on twelve crucial issues. Each of these matters is important for a good knowledge of salvation. The Bible presents us with a unified system of truth. Consequently, every doctrine is interwoven with every other doctrine in one whole coherent worldview. "The Scripture cannot be broken" (John 10:35).

First, we began by noting that God is a loving Creator. "He has made us and not we ourselves" (Psa 100:3). He tenderly created Adam as the progenitor of the human race, and he has created us for his glory and for our good. One of the foundational truths for understanding salvation is that which teaches that God is our Creator. The doctrine of creation is not simply an academic aside in our understanding of biblical doctrine, It is quite properly the very starting point of God's Word and all of its doctrines. Consequently, it is appropriate that we began our study here.

Secondly, we observed that when we look out into the world of human affairs, we see that man is a rebellious creature. The truth is that "God made men upright, but they have sought out many devices" (Eccl 7:29). The beautiful world and tender love that God gave to Adam in the beginning was rejected when Adam succumbed to the temptation to be like God (Gen 3:5). Man's highest aspiration is simultaneously his deepest sin: he sinfully longs to usurp the role of the Creator and arrogate to himself the right to determine good and evil. Because of the fall of Adam, we are all fallen in him (Rom 5:12ff). As fallen creatures we have rebelled against our loving God. Indeed, we are totally depraved, corrupt in every aspect of our being and wholly unable to please God.

Third, we studied the righteousness of God, noting that he is perfectly holy and righteous in his whole being and in all his ways. Since God lovingly created man and provided all that he needed, man's rebellion becomes a serious matter with God. As the infinitely righteous one, God must serve as the ultimate Judge of all men. Since his "eyes are too pure to approve evil" (Hab 1:13), he must deal with sin which has intruded into his earthly kingdom and corrupted his highest creature. Therefore he has "fixed a day in which He will judge the world in righteousness" (Acts 17:31). Men must understand that "we will all stand before the judgment seat of God" (Rom 14:10). And "it is a terrifying thing to fall into the hands of the living God" (Heb 10:31).

Fourth, we must take heart in recognizing that our loving Creator is also a gracious Redeemer. Though he is an offended God whose righteous wrath must be placated, he is also a loving God who provides redemption for his wayward creature. Since man is sinful to the very core of his being, God must provide the means of salvation, if man is to be saved from himself and from God's wrath. Indeed, from the very beginning when man fell (Gen 3:15), God set in motion a glorious plan of redemption that unfolds throughout Scripture until its completion in Christ when in "the fullness of the time . . . God sent forth His Son" that "He might redeem those who were under the Law" (Gal 4:4–5).

Fifth, we noted that Jesus Christ the Lord is God. Man's sin debt must be paid to an offended and holy God. But man is so sinful, he cannot pay that debt himself. Consequently, God sends his own Son, the Second Person of the Trinity, to secure redemption for us. The Son of God is not only perfectly holy but of infinite value so that he might placate God's wrath and redeem the vast multitude of God's elect. A core doctrine of the Christian faith, and a doctrine absolutely essential to our salvation, is that Jesus is "our Lord and our God" (John 20:28). He was in the beginning with God, because he was God (John 1:1).

Sixth, the Second Person of the Trinity takes upon himself a true human body and soul and enters into history. Since by his very nature God cannot suffer and die, he enters into history as one who is linked with both man and God, so that he might represent both in his redemptive transaction. As God in the flesh, he lives the perfect life that we should have lived. And as the God-man he is of infinite value so that he might stand in for an untold number of men. Indeed, "the Son of Man did not come to be served, but to serve, and to give His life a ransom for many" (Matt 20:28). He remains to this day in heaven above the fullness of Deity in bodily form (Col 2:9).

Seventh, God provides for man's salvation and offers it to him by faith alone. Once again, the very perfection of God and the deep imperfection of man make it impossible for man to do anything that will please God. And it is certainly impossible that he could do anything to secure his own redemption from the sin that brought him ruin. Whereas all other religions are moralistic, Christianity is a redemptive religion. Therefore, God brings salvation to man by his grace so that man might secure it by faith, which is itself a gift of God: "For by grace you have been saved through faith; and that not of yourselves, it is the gift of God; not as a result of works, so that no one may boast" (Eph 2:8–9). True faith, however, involves both a confident trust in God as well as holy repentance from sin.

Eighth, we saw that salvation is necessarily a life changer. Since men are dead in trespasses and sin (Eph 2:1), they need new (spiritual) life. Consequently, salvation is spoken of as a new birth (John 3:3; 1 Pet 1:23), as a passing from death into life (John 5:24; 1 John 3:14), as a new creation (2 Cor 5:17; Gal 6:15), and more. By the very nature of salvation's involving a new life principle, those truly born again will tend to live out the implications of their new life. Though salvation is free, it is not cheap. The true Christian has the Spirit within who moves him to live for God (Rom 8:4; Phil 2:12–13). Though we will not be perfect until we enter heaven, the Christian will tend to live for God.

Ninth, we noted that salvation is eternally secure. Salvation saves and it keeps. Our salvation brings us *eternal* life, which by the very nature of the case must last eternally. Thus, Jesus promises that "I give eternal life to them, and they will never perish; and no one will snatch them out of My hand" (John 10:29). Paul teaches us that "He who began a good work in you will perfect it until the day of Christ Jesus" (Phil 1:6). Salvation begins a good work in us; it will be continued until the end. Paul even dramatically notes "that neither death, nor life, nor angels, nor principalities, nor things present, nor things to come, nor powers, nor height, nor depth, nor any other created thing, will be able to separate us from the love of God, which is in Christ Jesus our Lord" (Rom 8:39).

Tenth, as a consequence of all of these great truths, we learned that Christians have a glorious destiny. A glorious future lies before us as the church makes progress in the world. Jesus promises that it will grow to a place of dominance, like the mustard seed grows to become a great plant (Matt 13:31–32). We are not on the losing side in history. Nor do we as individuals dwell on earth for "seventy years, / Or if due to strength, eight years" (Psa 90:10), and then die and vanish away. Rather, we have the hope of entering into heaven with God immediately upon the point of our death (2 Cor 5:8; Phil 1:23). Still further, we discovered that when history comes to an end, we will enter into a new earth in our resurrected bodies, so that we might dwell there forever serving God without sin (2 Pet 3:10–13).

Eleventh, because of God's great blessing to us we are obliged to tell others of his mercy and love. God uses his people as instruments in the salvation of others. He uses ordinary means to bring the extraordinary blessings of salvation to sinners. He calls us to preach the Word so that others may hear and be saved (Rom 10:14–15). Since men are sinners living under the wrath of God (John 3:36) they need the very gospel that saved us from our sins (Acts 2:40). God saves us and leaves us in this world that we might promote his will among the nations (Matt 5:13–16). Since salvation brings honor and glory to his name (Eph 1:5–13), our greatest service of God is that we tell others of his grace.

Twelfth, we finally learned that the Christian faith that brings salvation is an absolutely certain faith. We should be comforted to know that the Christian faith is an unassailable truth. We are committed to the self-sufficient God (Exo 3:14; John 5:26) who alone accounts for reality, logic, morality, and meaning in the world (Col 1:17; Heb 1:3). Not only so, but this should encourage us as we go forth, in that we have the answers to man's deepest need and his most fundamental questions.

As Christians we can have great confidence in life, because we know *The Truth about Salvation*.

NOTES

The Truth about SALVATION

A Study Guide for
Individual or Group Bible Study

Kenneth L. Gentry, Jr., Th.D.

Chesnee, South Carolina 29323
"Proclaiming the kingdom of God and teaching those things which concern
the Lord Jesus Christ, with all confidence."
(Acts 28:31)

The Truth about Salvation
A Study Guide for Individual or Group Bible Study
© Copyright 2019 by Gentry Family Trust udt April 2, 1999

All rights reserved. No part of this book may be reproduced in any form or by any means, except for brief quotations for the purpose of review, comment, or scholarship, without written permission from the publisher.

Unless otherwise noted, Scripture references are taken from the New American Standard Bible, © 1960, 1962, 1963, 1968, 1971, 1972, 1973, 1975, 1977, 1995 by The Lockman Foundation. Used by permission.

Published by:
Victorious Hope Publishing
P.O. Box 285
Chesnee, South Carolina 29323

Website: www.VictoriousHope.com

Printed in the United States of America

Cover design by Brian Godawa
Proof-reading by Bill Boney

ISBN 978-0-9964525-6-4

Victorious Hope Publishing is committed to producing Christian educational materials for promoting the whole Bible for the whole of life. We are conservative, evangelical, and Reformed and are committed to the doctrinal formulation found in the Westminster Standards.

www.ingramcontent.com/pod-product-compliance
Lightning Source LLC
Chambersburg PA
CBHW070811100426
42742CB00012B/2330